Contents

I0425202

Acknowledgements

To the eyewitnesses who've bravely come forward, telling us of apparent living pterosaurs, I dedicate this book. They deserve to be heard.

Several Americans have assisted investigations of what we call the "ropen," including three pioneers. Jim Blume, a missionary in Papua New Guinea for decades, interviewed dozens of native eyewitnesses of pterosaur-like creatures. Carl Baugh led the first three expeditions, preparing the way for the rest of us to follow. Paul Nation, in four expeditions, searched in two areas of that country, contracting serious infections twice.

Just weeks after my 2004 expedition on Umboi Island, the cryptozoologists Garth Guessman and David Woetzel interviewed Umboi native eyewitnesses with systematic interview forms (and those two Americans later assisted investigations in another country). Woetzel and I later wrote separate scientific papers, in a peer-reviewed journal, about our experiences in Papua New Guinea and about pterosaurs in human times. We appreciate the support from our families and from our friends here and abroad.

In the United States of America—that's where Scott Norman, in 2007, became the first American cryptozoologist to see a clear form of a living pterosaur while searching for one: a large flying creature with a head three to four feet long. We mourn the passing (from natural causes) of our young friend who is deeply missed in the cryptozoology community.

I give special thanks to Duane Hodgkinson, whose unflinching testimony gave birth to modern living-pterosaur investigations. His account of the 1944 sighting on the mainland of Papua New Guinea helped inspire Carl Baugh's first expedition of 1993. Ignoring previous ridicule from those who would not listen, Hodgkinson told us of his experience, helping prepare the way for many expeditions in the southwest Pacific. Alongside countless other American veterans of World War II, who risked their lives to preserve our freedom, he faced the threat of death in a faraway land. But his bravery in reporting a giant living "pterodactyl" gave us another freedom, even the freedom to believe in a life thought to have been long extinct—giant featherless long-tailed flying creatures, both faraway and here in America: live pterosaurs.

4

Live Pterosaurs in America

Eyewitness Reports of Pterosaurs in the Contiguous United States

By Jonathan David Whitcomb

Reports of huge flying "pterodactyls" in American skies have floated around the internet for years; but before about 2005, details were scarce. When an eyewitness was named, the interviewer was often anonymous; even when an eyewitness was credible, and the account published in a newspaper, the story was ridiculed, discouraging others who had also seen strange flying creatures. Where could eyewitnesses go? What a predicament for them! Who would believe their reports?

Since the two *ropen* expeditions of 2004, in Papua New Guinea, more Americans have learned of the living-pterosaur investigations and the many resulting eyewitness interviews. Many web pages have sprung up, many of them by explorers themselves. But despite other web pages, by scornful critics who never went anywhere and never interviewed anyone, those two expeditions, and those that preceded and followed them, are causing an awakening, opening human minds in the birth of a new perspective: Universal pterosaur extinction has been an assumption; some pterosaur species are still living. The author, one of those American explorers who interviewed natives in Papua New Guinea, has been interviewing American eyewitnesses since 2004.

How are sightings in the United States related to those in the southwest Pacific? How do some apparent nocturnal pterosaurs pertain to bats, and how are bats irrelevant? How could modern living pterosaurs have escaped scientific notice? These mysteries have slept in the dark, beyond the knowledge of almost all Americans, even beyond our wildest dreams (although the reality of some pterosaurs is a living nightmare to some bats). These mysteries have slept . . . until now.

Cover: San Joaquin Wildlife Sanctuary, Irvine, California, with sketch by Eskin Kuhn, eyewitness of two pterosaurs seen in Cuba in 1971

Introduction

This book might make a few Americans uneasy to walk alone at night; my intention, however, is not to frighten but to enlighten as many readers as possible to know about live-pterosaur investigations. Those who've been shocked at the sight of a flying creature that "should" be extinct—those eyewitnesses, more numerous than most Americans would guess, need no longer be afraid that everyone will think them crazy, and no longer need they feel alone. Those of us who've listened to the American eyewitnesses, we who have interviewed them, we now believe. So, if you will, consider the experiences of these ordinary persons (I've interviewed most of them myself) and accept whatever enlightenment you may.

This book might discomfort, even offend, a few readers; please consider the feelings of those who have revealed to us their encounters with what seem to be live pterosaurs, for some of them have suffered more than discomfort. I intend to comfort those innocent victims who have been ridiculed or ostracized because of a cultural weakness, for each has seen something unaccepted by their society. Each eyewitness deserves listeners who will open their minds, really listen. Consider their experiences.

If this book does nothing more than comfort the eyewitnesses of strange creatures, I would be grateful; but there's much more. We need to understand why we believe what we believe. When I first began researching these eyewitness sightings, years ago, I mentioned a word to a kindergartner: "pterosaurs;" he said, "A comet." Years later, while writing this book, I mentioned my work to a second-grader; she said, "Who will buy your book? Crazy people?" I think better of you. And I think, because of what she and many others have told me, that we must understand indoctrination, for it influences our beliefs; the extent of that influence discomforts me.

My American associates and I who have explored in Papua New Guinea, searching for living pterosaurs, intend no deceit; we intend only enlightenment. Ten expeditions, within sixteen years, have rewarded us with many eyewitness accounts and video evidence for what we believe is the bioluminescence of a flying creature; but we still lack a clear photo of a pterosaur. We have been labeled foolish, biased, and crazy; but the few who say "lies" reveal their own foolishness: Why would we work so hard, for so long, with so many opportunities to fabricate pterosaur sightings in so many remote jungles, and then admit that we never saw any clear form of a pterosaur? It is because we intend not to deceive but to enlighten.

On Umboi Island, I led the first of the two expeditions of 2004, with two other American cryptozoologists following a few weeks later. Six native eyewitnesses (among many) we interviewed with amazing results: Three men saw, at Lake Pung, a giant featherless long-tailed flying creature in daylight; three other men saw similar large-to-giant creatures but glowing at night or at twilight. If reports were only from Umboi, only from six eyewitnesses, and only from natives, we might doubt, but there's more.

On the Papua New Guinea mainland, in 2006, Paul Nation and his associate, native minister Jacob Kepas, explored deep in the highland interior. One night, Paul videotaped two glowing objects at the top of a ridge. The natives attribute this kind of light to large flying creatures that used to carry away pigs and children from their village.

In daylight, Jacob was led up a mountain where he thought he could just make out the features of a large winged-creature sleeping on a cliff; his guide then climbed higher, confirming it was the creature called "indava."

Early in 2007, Paul Nation's video footage was analyzed by a physicist. That recording of the two lights could not be enhanced to reveal any form of what produced them, but detailed analysis revealed that they were not from any camp fires, lanterns, car headlights, meteors, or airplanes; also, the lights were not camera artifacts or the result of a paste-on hoax. Both lights were consistent: made by real objects on that remote ridge.

At about the time the physicist was analyzing those two lights, an expedition team called *Destination Truth* (for the Sci-Fi channel) videotaped a flying light similar to what Paul had videotaped. It was flying near the coast of the mainland of Papua New Guinea. The video footage was analyzed, in the United States, by two forensic video experts; they could not explain the light. Natives on that east coast of the mainland of Papua New Guinea had told the explorers that the lights are made by large flying creatures.

During those years of expeditions in the southwest Pacific, reports in our own country became impossible to ignore; I received many emails from eyewitnesses across the United States, and the reports kept coming in. Pterosaur-like creatures are not all confined to the tropics. As we began to listen to those Americans, we noticed report-similarities: long tails (often) and apparent bioluminescence (sometimes). We began to believe.

These flying creatures, apparent pterosaurs seen by eyewitnesses in Papua New Guinea, in America, and in other countries, have not yet been captured or clearly photographed, so they're still classified not in zoology textbooks but in cryptozoology. . . . still . . . you be the judge.

Chapter 1

South Carolina Sighting

Susan Wooten was driving east on Highway 20, to the town of Florence, on a clear mid-afternoon in the fall of about 1989, following a girl who lived in her dorm, who was driving ahead. Where the road was surrounded by woods and swamps, Wooten saw something flying from her left, then passing in front of her, behind her friend's car. "It swooped down over the highway and back up gracefully over the pines," but its appearance was shocking: "It looked as big as any car . . . NO feathers, not like a huge crane or egret, but like a humongous bat."

She pulled over, as did others who'd been driving in the other direction, but she had no time to talk with other eyewitnesses: Her friend had seen nothing (for it had flown behind her) and continued driving away.

Local libraries revealed other sighting accounts in the area, but not until 2007 did Wooten find much more: accounts on web sites, including my own pages. We started an online interview that continued into 2008. But something distinguished our interviews from many other interviews involving sightings in North America. After months of answering my questions, she remembered a different kind of sighting in South Carolina, at first seemingly unrelated: strange flying lights in a swamp.

She began answering my questions on October 21, 2007:

Q: How many feet above the highway was it?

A: Probably 20 feet or so. It started out above pine treetops and swooped lower . . . and up again to fly up above treetops on the other side [right].

Q: Were the wings flapping?

A: One or two slow flaps, to the best of my recollection.

Q: What was the approximate distance from wingtip to wingtip?

A: My best guess is 12-15 feet.

Q: Could you make a sketch of the creature?

A: Oh yes.

I wrote, "Thank you very much for letting me know about this."

She replied, "Thank you . . . Just that someone else has seen what I have is nice . . . I hate when people think I am crazy . . . I know what I saw. . . ."

I continued the questions:

Q: What highway number was it? . . . closer to Columbia or Florence?

A: Hwy 20 going from Columbia to Florence . . . about 2/3 to 3/4 of the way to Florence. Columbia is a major (for us) city, but as soon as you leave it, it is nothing but woods, sand, lots of pine forests, and moves quickly into swamps.

Q: From your answer to [earlier questioning], it seems to me that the flight of the creature was between perpendicular to the highway and parallel to the highway. Is that correct?

A: It was crossing perpendicularly to the highway—left to right, or north-south . . . crossing from one piney area to the other across the hwy.

Q: Do you remember anything about the weather?

A: Nice pretty day—clear, in the fall, but don't remember which month.

Q: Do you remember anything about the color of the creature?

A: Darkish is about all I can say . . . can't remember that . . . it was so much to take in at once—so startling.

Q: Would you be so kind as to make a sketch and mail it to me?

A: Will do!!! And thanks again.

Wooten then wrote to me about a different kind of sighting:

"I have a footnote, possibly of interest. Once I typed these answers, I went to your website and read . . . I was intrigued by the fact that some of these 'ropens' give off a luminescence at night. It made me think of when I was in college. We had a group that would often travel to Bingham, nearby. (Never even connected these things together, if in fact they could be.) There was an old abandoned stretch of railway leading into the swamp where we would . . . see the 'Bingham Lights.' No one knew what they were . . . Anyway, the 'ghost story' was that there was some poor ghost with a lantern looking for his head or some such nonsense . . . fun enough for college kids to gather (often 15 or 20 at a time) to go watch. . . . It never failed, when we'd go, that we would see this phenomenon. It was actually pretty scary a few times, the lights coming fearfully close to us, enough that we'd jump into our cars and leave."

"So, whatever this information is worth . . . Bingham is about a 15-minute drive from Francis Marion College, and from Florence, but I forget just which way—but it's nearby.

"Hope this helps and is not just a waste of time. . . .

Susan Wooten"

Wooten sketched the creature she had seen flying over the highway. "Definitely no feathers—this thing was not only huge but was practically on top of me—maybe 20 ft. (?) above & 25 ft. (?) in front of me."

From the end of October into November, we continued. I wrote:

"Thank you again. Regarding the Bingham Lights . . . more questions"

Q: Have you (or anyone you know of) heard any sound associated with the Bingham Lights, when they come close?

A: No sounds.

Q: How high above the ground are the lights?

A: They were from 8-10 feet to maybe 15 feet, not high—it's in the swamp. (Water oaks and cypress and such have low reaching branches) . . . beneath the branches, above the water.

Q: You mentioned "jump into our cars." Can [you] drive into the swamp?

A: We drove down the old railway line where the tracks no longer exist, parked, got out at this opening . . . where the tracks crossed at a crossway type area, then walked . . . a tressle-like hump that the opposing railway used to travel. It was perhaps 15 or so feet wide but extended deep into the swamp . . . maybe 30-50 yards . . . before ending abruptly. . . . I know, because I walked to the end of it myself once. You couldn't take a car out onto this trestle, it was too rounded, too narrow. Too old and unstable. But you could walk it. . . .

Q: Is there any color to the lights?

A: No, clear, as in a flashlight. Only much larger . . . about a foot or so across in diameter.

Q: Do the lights fly straight or do they change course often?

A: They mostly flew straight, but saw them once, maybe twice, change direction.

Q: Do the lights ever change speed?

A: No, not that I recall . . . about the same each time. If it seemed different, I thought that it was due to the distance from us . . .

Q: Do the lights flicker in any way?

A: No, it never did. More of a glowing steady light. Like a live force, I don't know how to explain this. But a clear light as in a flashlight, but not as concentrated, or bright . . . sort of in a ball shape. It was spooky. It did come close enough to be a "threat" . . . by that I mean, we all felt extremely vulnerable to whatever this light could do to us if it "wanted to" . . . we did get scared truly several times, because it seemed the light (or lights) could shift towards us . . . But being a college student, somewhat learned, I decided that this had to be some type of swamp gas. (Check out Clemson University—I remember that there were rumors that they had come down and ruled out swamp gas . . . so maybe check them out.)

Q: Have you heard about why the railroad lines were in the swamp?

A: No, just that they were very old. [end of this line of questioning]

Early in 2008, I recounted Wooten's experiences to an associate living-pterosaur investigator (who generally prefers anonymity). Here are excerpts of his communications with her: [investigator SMW]

"Susan, Hello. I am an acquaintance of Jonathan Whitcomb and a field researcher for an organization studying living pterosaurs. . . . thank you for reporting your sighting. I know it takes a lot of courage to talk about . . . people so often don't believe . . . I've been researching living pterosaurs for about seven years. . . . and conducted several expeditions. . . .

"[What] I thought most interesting was . . . the Bingham lights. As you heard from Jonathan, the people from Papua New Guinea say . . . [the pterosaurs] glow at night. The few times I've been able to see [what the investigators believe to be pterosaurs], while doing field research, have always been at night, and I can definitely say that they really do produce a light. The light isn't always on, but when they turn it on, it can be a brief flash or a longer lasting glow." [end of email from SMW]

Here are excerpts of Susan's replies to the questions from the researcher:

[Regarding daylight sighting over the highway] "I am glad that you got in touch with me. . . . It is not something I freely tell anyone, as they think I am either lying or plumb crazy—but I know what I saw."

[Regarding the *Bingham Lights*] "We saw sometimes only one light, and other times many lights (once up to four, [or] more). The lights were . . . always moving, and each was the same size."

She included one especially frightening encounter with a *Bingham Light*:

"We were walking down this "peninsula" thing . . . maybe six or eight of us, and we got about halfway down it when the light came straight for us, I think about 8-10 feet over our heads . . . went over us (we all ducked, mind you, some screaming) and continued on over us and away behind us. It was extremely terrifying, considering we knew not what it was nor what it was capable of doing to us. Well, some idiot (not with our group—one of the other people gathered [there], we did not know) shot at it with what sounded like a .22 . . . now we not only had a strange and possibly dangerous ball of light nearby . . . we had a certified lunatic with a gun . . . to me, at that time, I could not decide which was more dangerous—was leaning towards the guy with the gun—but also there was the main problem of where to go: to the drop-off at the end, away from the gun but further into nowhere land, or to one side? I finally scrambled down one side of the track and held my position until I heard commotion and cars leaving . . . so we got back to our cars and left as well."

After months of email interviews, I became convinced that Susan was a credible eyewitness. I believe she saw something like a *ropen*—probably a *Rhamphorhynchoid* pterosaur—that flew in front of her car. The overall communications we have had are inconsistent with both a hoax and a mental health condition. Her descriptions of the creature, and the closeness of the encounter, repudiate a misidentification of a bird or bat.

Could it have been a giant mechanical model? This mechanical idea breaks down. Why would a model fly from one swamp into another swamp? Why would it be so much bigger than the known mechanical models? How could it dive down to just above the highway and then ascend to fly over trees tops on the other side, without any acceleration of wing flapping and without even any mechanical appearance of wing flapping? And why would a mechanical model closely resemble a giant flying creature that catches fish on reefs in Papua New Guinea? They're both too much alive.

What about the *Bingham Lights*? With so much room for speculation, and so many places for an unclassified nocturnal flying creature to hide, and so many reports of flying lights in the United States, I think that "flying luminescence" deserves a chapter of its own. But I'll summarize here: The *Bingham Lights* of South Carolina resemble the *ropen* lights of Papua New Guinea more than they resemble swamp gas or any other commonplace explanation; they're uncommon: maybe, just maybe, *ropens*.

Chapter 2
California Sightings

When I returned from Papua New Guinea, in 2004, I knew almost nothing about reports of apparent pterosaurs, or "dragons," in California. I was convinced of the reality of long-tailed *ropens* of the southwest Pacific, but assumed they live there because of the vast tropical wildernesses, providing them warmth, food, and seclusion. I also assumed that the few reports that I had read—apparent pterosaurs in some of the 48 States—were of a few stragglers from Central America. But after publishing many web pages about living pterosaurs in Papua New Guinea, I received emails and phone calls from eyewitnesses: sightings in California, Texas, New Mexico, Oklahoma, Arkansas, Florida, Georgia, South Carolina, North Carolina, Virginia, Maryland-Virginia border, Pennsylvania, New York, Rhode Island, Ohio, Kentucky, Indiana, Michigan, Wisconsin, Kansas, and Washington State. I became a believer in American pterosaurs.

The greatest danger facing innovators, rebels, and those who search for living pterosaurs—that's a newspaper. National newspapers ignored the success of the Wright brothers (their December, 1903, successful powered flight at Kitty Hawk, North Carolina). News reporters and editors, many of them, assumed that the controlled powered-flight of two bicycle mechanics was a lie, that it never happened. Even as late as 1908, many newspaper professionals thought the Wright brothers "better liars than flyers." After all, a well-funded government-sponsored flying machine had crashed only a few days before the Wright brothers were said to have first flown. But lack of news reporting and abundance of lie-insinuations can relate to both flying machines and flying pterosaurs, even those called "dragons."

But flying dragons! In modern California? Without news headlines? It's easier to believe in flying bicycle mechanics. But just a few years before newspapers were ignoring (or accusing) the Wright brothers on the East Coast, they were indeed reporting accounts of flying "pterodactyls" on the West Coast. And they used that same careless word, the cheap label that would soon be thrown at the bicycle mechanics: "liar."

Cryptozoology author Chad Arment wrote "The Pterodactyls of Fresno County, California" for the *BioFortean Review* (November 2006, No. 5). I include a summary of those newspaper accounts here, and suggest that they should not be summarily dismissed, every one. I cannot prove all the accounts were genuine, for they were recorded secondhand in the early 1890's. I suggest that at least some eyewitnesses were telling the truth, regardless of the opinions of the news reporters of that time, and that at least some eyewitnesses may have seen a living pterosaur. I do not submit these old reports as indisputable evidence to prove pterosaurs lived in the late nineteenth century; I submit them to dismiss any potential objection that twentieth century and twenty-first century reports of living pterosaurs in California are without historical precedence: Sightings continue.

In the summer of 1891, southeast of Fresno, several eyewitnesses reported two featherless flying creatures with wingspans of fifteen feet. Reportedly reputable residents around Reedley described the two "dragons" for the newspaper: broad heads, long bills, and large eyes. "On the night of July 11 . . . their peculiar cries and the rustling of their mammoth wings were heard as late as 10 o'clock." Two nights later, the "monsters" were held responsible for attacking chickens, with "many of the hens being bitten in two and left partly devoured." On the following week, a carriage of pic- nickers saw the creatures "plainly circling in the air." Two days later, two men saw them fly up from under a bridge, passing close enough that the men felt the wind from the flapping.

"Scientific investigators" from Fresno came to hunt the creatures, hiding in holes specially dug for hiding (how they knew where to hide I know not). When the creatures arrived, they were reportedly seen to have, not bills like birds, "snouts resembling that of an alligator." After the creatures dived into the water, the wings appeared like "large knobs on their backs." Teeth were visible; the eyes never blinked. A few mudhens were caught and devoured, one of them "in two or three clamps of the jaws."

The newspapers in surrounding towns then ridiculed the reports. (But now, because of those old newspapers, we know of those reports, so don't burn old newspapers.) Much that was written in the articles was in response to previous reports, so errors may have crept in. Maybe residents of Reedley really did see live pterosaurs. Those descriptions given by the "scientific investigators," at least, do seem consistent with modern ideas about how some pterosaurs would appear.

Regardless, news people are, above all else, people: human bias, even in news professionals, can cause one to ridicule the seemingly ridiculous. And while humans gossip about the kind of whiskey neighbors are drink- ing, maybe, just maybe, two pterosaurs are devouring a few mudhens.

Internet reports of twentieth century sightings in California—these can easily be copied from one web page to another, without sign of original source. A "couple driving through Trinity National Forest" (Northern California) in the 1960's may have been a real couple, but how are we to know? The pterodactyl-like creature may have had a wingspan of 14 feet, but who interviewed the couple? Who verified that they were real persons? Even an anonymous eyewitness needs to have an interviewer, like me, to link to the sighting. In cryptozoology, trying to verify something is really a pterosaur is secondary; primary is verifying an eyewitness is a real human.

I was delighted when a lady told me, in mid-2007, about a sighting she had around 1991 in a Southern California desert. After buying a copy of my book *Searching for Ropens*, she had asked the publisher for my contact information. Two years after our emails began, I spoke with her by phone, verifying her credibility.

"Dear Mr. Whitcomb [email of June 25, 2007]

"I have been haunted for close to twenty years by what I saw in the desert. I have never told anyone due to the fact that I was afraid I would be thought nuts. [The other eyewitness] was in the public eye and did not want to be ridiculed. Anyway I can't tell you what a relief it is to know I am not alone. If you would like more information on what I saw you can email me . . . Thank you again for helping me to deal with this. Sincerely [MB]"

Q: What desert was this? [My questioning began June 26th, by email]

A: The [Anza-Borrego] State Park. We did four-wheel-drive everywhere we went in the three days we were out there. We would pack our provisions and head out at dawn and would not return to base until close to sundown. I wasn't the driver and I had never been out there before so I will do the best I can to recall. I do remember traveling in the Badlands. . . . I also recall Henderson Canyon Trail. I remember this because we checked out Peg Leg Smith's Historical Marker. . . . The day we saw the animal I believe we were somewhere between Old Kane Springs and the Badlands. The man I was with got rather freaked when he saw the creature and wanted to go back to base. I believe we left for home the following morning.

Q: What time of year was it?

A: It was approximately 16 years ago [1991] that I had the sighting but I'll dig deep. To the best of my recollection it was in the spring . . . I am not sure. . . . it was not in the summer. I don't do well in the heat.

Q: What time of day was it?

A: Late afternoon, almost sundown.

Q: How well did you see the form or shape of the creature?

A: Well enough to remember some details and to never forget what I saw. We were sitting in the late afternoon shade of a ridge, on lawn chairs, enjoying the solitude and peace and quiet of the desert when it passed over. I caught the sight of it with the corner of my eye and looked up. It was soaring along the side of a plateau not far from us. We knew what it looked like. In fact, I remember saying '. . . that looks just like a Taradactyl!'

"My friend looked in the binoculars and said it looked like one but it had to be a kite or something because they were extinct. (We saw a total of two people, both men in their 30's, in the three days. I doubt seriously if someone was out in the middle of nowhere flying a kite.)

"I grabbed the binoculars and looked for myself. What I saw was large and very much alive. Its hue was close to the hue of the desert sand but more the color of rust. Its skin, I say skin because there were no feathers, . . . looked like dull leather sort of dusty looking. It seemed to soar like a large raptor. The back of the head was pointed.

"By the time I got the binoculars, it was moving away from me, so I didn't get a good look at the face, but it seemed to be narrow and mostly beak. It did move its wings slowly down and up once when it turned slightly to head into another canyon where we lost sight of it. It did not have a tail. But it did have a nub where a tail would be.

"When we first saw it, we thought that it was about the size of an eagle. But after we talked about it, we realized it just seemed smaller due to the desert landscape. When we started making comparisons, we knew it had to have been [a] lot larger than an eagle, maybe three times larger.

"By now my companion was getting very agitated and nervous. He wanted to be out of that part of the canyon before it became totally dark. I didn't want to go. I guess my excitement and curiosity took over my better judgement. Maybe I should of been afraid, it certainly looked big and scary. I just didn't feel any fear of it. Sincerely, [MB]"

Later, MB sent me another email.

"Hello, Jonathan:

". . . something . . . happened when I went back out to the desert approximately one year from the original sighting. After reading your book, what I saw the second time may be relevant to the first sighting.

"My now-ex-husband and I took a camping trip to Anza [Borrego] Desert and camped in an area we called Coyote Canyon. . . late at night . . . we were sitting in lawn chairs up against our camper. [He] said, "Look over there, what is that!" I looked and what I saw was a bright red light just hovering over the hill that was closest to us. It moved along the hill, then it moved up a little higher. I thought that it was going to take off like UFO's are reported to do. But it didn't. It slowly moved in a downward motion until it was out of sight. Soon after it disappeared behind the hill, I was in the camper scared to death that we had a UFO encounter. Larry was very excited because he believed that we did . . . experience a UFO sighting. I didn't know what I had seen, but whatever it was, it was awe inspiring. I wanted to leave but he wanted to stay, so we stayed. I didn't sleep all night because I was so frightened. Sincerely, [MB]"

I considered the possibility that the red light may have come from the same creature this lady had seen one year earlier; But I had doubt. Not until the American-pterosaur investigations of 2007 and 2008 did I come to a firm belief in bioluminescent *ropen*-like creatures in the United States.

In July of 2008, I received a phone call from a man who reported a very large flying creature, seen one year earlier, in Orange County, less than one mile north of the University of California at Irvine. He described the dark gray or black animal as 30 feet long, with 15-16 feet of that being a tail. He saw the creature fly "at low altitude," in front of his car, over the road (Campus Drive), into the San Joaquin Wildlife Sanctuary.

SNW (anonymous) had no view of any feet and no good view of the head. He noticed that during the creature's flight the tail was straight, as if it was "stretched out to be measured." A flange, close to the end of the tail, he described as "triangle-shaped."

The wings had "wrinkles" on the underside, showing absence of feathers. Flapping frequency was about two seconds per flap; he later elaborated: 0.75 seconds up-wing, 0.75 seconds down-wing. And the creature looked wet, as if it had just come out of the water.

I kept certain facts about the person and his testimony secret, as I did with other eyewitnesses. But anonymity of the eyewitness is only one reason for my secrecy. Until the *ropen* and other pterosaur-like creatures graduate from cryptozoology into zoology, until they are acknowledged and classified in scientific journals, investigators may be vulnerable to a hoax; therefore the reasonings behind my judgements of eyewitness credibility are often kept secret, to avoid making life too easy for hoaxers.

But I found SNW to be credible. It seemed unlikely to have been a hoax, hallucination, or misidentification. His reputation in his profession could only be damaged, were he to perpetrate a hoax, and that damage could be severe. His description of the creature and the manner of his describing it are inconsistent with hallucinating a giant pterosaur. The size and features, including a 15-foot tail, practically eliminate misidentification.

I realize that somebody may suggest the eyewitness saw only a model pterosaur; mechanical "pterodactyls" are common. Several details rule out this explanation. The size of the creature was estimated by its appearance when it flew over the road at low altitude; I doubt that he saw a 30-foot-long model. In addition, it was flying from a fenced-off marshy area off-limits to the general public; I doubt that any model-pterodactyl enthusiast would choose that marsh for launching a giant model. And why would a it be flown low over a road into a wooded area that was bordered by tall buildings? Its hard to imagine a worse place to fly a model. Only ideal launching and landing places would justify the expense of building a giant model airplane; this place had neither. Other factors eliminate this model-explanation, but I later found out why a living *ropen* might fly there.

I visited the San Joaquin Wildlife Sanctuary but without hope of having my own sighting, for that *ropen* could have flown to South America or Canada in the past year. I found the road the eyewitness had described and took photos (he later verified that the location photographed was correct).

Interacting with humans who were walking on the trails of the sanctuary, I hoped somebody had seen or heard something relevant. A few hikers were willing to answer my questions. If only I had lost a dog; I could then have asked, "Have you seen a Cocker Spaniel?" I could not ask, "Have you seen a thirty-foot long *Rhamphorhynchoid* pterosaur?" Just try that to start a conversation with a stranger.

I eventually found a reasonable question: "Have you seen or heard of anything very unusual flying here, something larger than the common birds?"

Delighted to have formulated a question that allowed me to appear non-crazy, I started conversations with hikers; but they were ignorant.

One man asked me a question or two. I tried to avoid getting into details that might make me appear batty, but I also had to keep an open mind to the chance that he had seen something. As he was leaving to walk down a trail, he asked, "like a baby pterodactyl?" I replied, "Something like that." He smiled and walked away; apparently he had seen nothing. It reminded me that sometimes nothing I can say will allow me to appear normal: It's only the nature of my work . . . I hope it's only that.

A few weeks later, I took my wife and two of our daughters to the wild-life sanctuary (the eyewitness told me he would not even consider going in there). With family, I don't need to pretend to be something I am not: normal. I took more photos as we walked to the far northwest area that is open to the public. This is where the creature was heading after it crossed the road a year earlier. We found a meadow where the creature could have landed: not visible from the road but a reasonable place for it to land.

I received an email, in October of 2009, from a man who had been search-ing the internet for urban hiking trails around Orange County. He found one of my web pages about the San Joaquin Wildlife Sanctuary and the giant flying creature that had flown over the road; it reminded him of what he had experienced around 1997. I will not classify the experience of OMF as a "sighting," but I believe that it was a real encounter. He is credible.

"I never considered that there could be a prehistoric creature still living today, but I had an experience about 12-years ago that has nearly changed my mind; it has at least made me consider it.

"I was living at the time in Rancho Santa Margarita, which is a master planned community near the O'Neal Canyons and the foothills of Saddle-back mountain range.

"My house was on the perimeter of the community, one backyard from the road that separates the wilderness canyons from the community. We had lived there about 10-years and never had seen anything except for some hawks, coyotes, and rabbits.

"One night I was awakened at about 1:00 a.m., with the most . . . awful screeching and screaming that I have ever heard. It sounded like . . . pigs being slaughtered, . . . like some sort of creature was suffering, or fighting for its life in my backyard.

"The sound was so terrifying that the hair stood up all over my body as I went to the window in my bedroom which faced Northeast towards the canyons and mountains. I opened the curtains and tried to see into the dark night. I opened the window hoping to get a better gauge on where the sound was coming from . . .

"I could make out that the sound was accompanied by some thrashing around in some hedges or bushes in the backyard of my . . . neighbors house, which was vacant at the time. The unearthly screeching continued and it almost sounded like there was a struggle to the death going on.

"I woke my wife who for some reason was sleeping through the noise. I asked her what she thought it was; she said it sounded like a dog or cat being killed; she was wrong.

"I could not stop myself from going downstairs to investigate more closely. When I got to the dining room and the door that led to the backyard, my fear got the better of me and instead I went to the front door and went out into the dark.

"I went into the front yard and stood there for a minute listening, trying to hear if the sound was still going on; it had stopped. I then moved cautiously towards the driveway on the side of the house and waited and strained to hear again. As I stood silent, I heard what I would describe as a call, a short screeching bark; it came from the back of the house where the previous noise had come from.

"Chills shot up and down my spine. As I stood holding my breath, I heard a deep, soft 'hushing' sound, like giant wings lifting something heavy into the air. This came from around the side of my house, in-between my house and the next-door-neighbors house.

"I was transfixed with fear . . . but I didn't 'see' so much as 'felt' it. Whatever it was, swept up and onto the chimney of the next-door-neighbors house. The night sky was incredibly dark so I could not really make out anything, but a large hulking 'presence' sat on that chimney. As I stared hard into the dark, trying to make out a shape or a movement, I realized whatever it was was staring right back at me.

"I left the yard quickly and went inside. . . . I didn't sleep well that night.

"The next day I called around and finally got a hold of a wild-animal control center in Orange County. I described what I had heard and experienced; they told me that it was mostly likely a Great Horned owl.

"I never bought that and somewhere in the recesses of my consciousness I cannot get the image of a large prehistoric featherless bird standing about four and a half feet tall, balanced on a chimney, staring at me in the dark.

"By the way, I have read the account of the San Joaquin Wildlife sighting and that is only about 20-miles from where I lived when this happened.

"Thanks for listening." [OMF]

Since this eyewitness had the name of a prominent business executive in Orange County, I phoned his office to confirm that he was the one who had emailed me. (I have no desire to be the victim of a hoaxer impersonating someone else.) I was delighted to learn that it was no hoax, for he confirmed the Rancho Santa Margarita encounter. Nobody in his position would perpetrate a hoax with a story like that.

I realize that, of all the possible-pterosaur-encounter reports that I have published, this one may have the least evidential value; the man actually saw practically nothing; he heard it. Nevertheless, it fits into the overall picture of a giant flying creature. We would expect some vague non-sighting encounters (hearing something strange rather than seeing it) and this may be one of them. Weak, yes; indirect, yes; but the descriptions of the sounds are detailed, potentially useful to compare with other reports.

It reminded me of an email I received from a man who had a friend living on the island of Spetses, Greece. One night this friend was walking toward a bridge when he heard a loud breathing sound, louder than could be made by a human. As he came closer, he noticed that the breathing, like that of some huge animal that was sick, came from the under-structure of the bridge. After leaving the area, there was a loud screeching and something with a "huge wingspan" flew away. That encounter also involved sound more than sight, but let's return to California.

I received an email, in September of 2009, from a man who lives in the San Fernando Valley (northern Los Angeles County). RI titled his email "Possible Ropen sighting - Sherman Oaks, CA." This was purely visual.

"Hello Mr. Whitcomb

"I just wanted to let you know that my girlfriend and I saw a creature last night (9/21/2009) that baffled us. It was a very large, winged creature that was gliding maybe 100 yards above us. We stared at the creature in disbelief because it was so strange . . . it didn't look like a bird really. . . it almost didn't look alive until it beat its wings, once, before going out of view. I didn't have my best glasses on but my girlfriend has 20-20 vision and she told a few minutes later that it had lights on it. That didn't strike me as right so I asked her if she was sure and she said they weren't lights exactly, but that the wings had a glow or reflection. I wasn't sure what to make of that so when I got to work today I begin my search for "flying creature" on Google. One link led to another and eventually I discovered something known as a Ropen. That was it! The description matched exactly what we saw, down to the glow. This isn't a hoax, we really saw something strange last night and after finding your website by following Wikipedia, I had to let you know. The time was approximately 10:30 pm and the nearest cross streets were Burbank Blvd & Woodman in the city of Sherman Oaks, CA (Los Angeles County). Thanks for reading."

I gave RI a phone call on September 23, to ask questions and get a feel for his credibility. I asked, "How was it unlike a bird?" He replied that it was bigger, was not flapping its wings (he mentioned a lack of any breeze), and its wings were larger from leading edge to back of wings. He estimated the wingspan at ten to fifteen feet, mentioning that his girlfriends estimate was twenty feet. The wings were more bat-like than bird-like. He acknowledged the difficulty of size estimation in the dark.

The creature was flying southeast. It was too dark to see whether or not it had a tail. His girlfriend saw the creature before he did. RI's sighting lasted about twelve seconds; hers (according to him), about sixteen to seventeen. They were walking a dog, with no other apparent eyewitnesses. He had never before thought about the possibility of living pterosaurs. He told several people about it; the typical response, "What were you smoking?"

I soon phoned AG, the girlfriend of RI. She confirmed the sighting that lasted about ten seconds. She mentioned a hang-glider shape but was sure of an organic wing movement: It was no hang-glider, mostly gliding, but with flexible wings contracting in and out when they moved. It was too dark to see if there was a tail. She emphasized that the creature was big.

The glowing parts of the wing caught her attention, each wing having four or five fuzzy lights. They were not dots, but longer, not round.

They often walk in that area at about 10-10:30 at night, but had never seen anything like that before. After the sighting, while walking back, they talked about it, but she mentioned it to nobody else except her mother.

In April of 2010, RI told me about his coworker who also had a sighting: a glowing or shining "flying dinosaur." ASM responded to my email.

"It was late in the evening, almost dark . . . I was walking from my car to my house (Sun Valley) and something in the sky caught my eye. My girl-friend also looked up and right away said, "Is that a bat?" But she wears glasses so she has trouble seeing how close objects are. What caught my eye was the bright radiation like light coming from the belly of this Ptero-dactyl looking animal. I seen it fly right above us maybe 150-200 feet and this thing wasn't no bat; it was bigger with large wing span, and when it flapped its wings it was kind of a slow lazy flap kind of gliding through the air. The animal radiated light from the bottom like when something is wet and you flash a light on it the light reflects back and shimmers. . . . I only [saw it] for about 15-20 seconds and it was out of sight . . . it seemed to be going somewhere, not just gliding around. From what I remember, this thing [had] a wing span of about 15-20 feet; I can't be too sure because he was up in the clear sky: nothing I could really compare size to."

I believed those accounts of large glowing flying creatures because of the investigation of similar lights in the United States and because of my 2004-expedition interviews in Papua New Guinea (as well as interviews conducted by other investigators). Large bioluminescent flyers are real.

Over Campus Drive, it flew away and to the right, into the public area of the San Joaquin Wildlife Sanctuary. It was as long as the road is wide.

The flight destination may have been this meadow near Campus Drive.

One of many ponds in the San Joaquin Wildlife Sanctuary—here many birds (and a few bats) could feed a hungry ropen.

Chapter 3

Other U.S. Sightings

Encountering an apparent living pterosaur can be frightening. I received an eyewitness report, in 2006, about an incident in about 1986, in the northwest area of San Antonio, Texas. I'll call her "DF."

"One evening, I was outside my apartment building . . . talking to my brother. . . . We were very used to the normal nightly activities of the area. We knew what the local birds and bats looked like and were familiar with exotic animals as well, from regular zoo attendance and general interest. My dad and I had, on several occasions, noticed bats flying right near our heads . . . Neither my brother or I was prone to being scared by anything outside at night. This night was different.

"We noticed something flying around across the road from where we were. This is (or was at the time) a two-lane road, and the creature was flying just above the phone lines. It would go one direction, turn, and swoop back. The shape was wrong for any large bird of the area, and the size was much too large to be any bat I have ever seen (I have seen a *flying fox* in a zoo, too, once with wings spread). The wingspan was huge, anywhere from 6-10 feet across. We watched the thing for maybe twenty minutes or so and were both very sure that it was also watching us.

"I don't know how to describe to you the feeling that we both got, watching this thing flying so close to us. The longer we watched, the more spooked we became. It was as though a giant vampire bat (like Dracula-style) was there, but neither of us thought it really looked like a bat, either, even a big one. Also, all the bigger bats are fruit-eaters and not scary at all. This was frightening. I get little chills just writing about it now.

"Since that time, we have debated and discussed all sorts of possibilities about what we saw that night. I came across your [web site] after seeing others that mentioned pterosaur reports in the U.S. The fear we felt seems to be similar to what is reported in the witness statements from Papua New Guinea. Are there any other reports of these things in the U.S.?

"The threat felt from this thing is what bothers me the most. Once . . . I encountered a cougar . . . That did not scare me. This thing did. [DF]"

Through *Youtube* (I have uploaded videos about the *ropen*), in 2007, I found a lady who had a sighting in Texas, but it turned out to be this same eyewitness (DF). Nevertheless, she then provided more insight.

"I did see it, and this wasn't a model, though that [model pterodactyl] looks really cool. This was alive, and watching us, and very, very scary (& I don't scare easily). I love animals, and have seen many, many species of birds, both in the wild and in zoos (San Antonio Zoo does have a great collection of birds). I adore owls and birds of prey, and am very familiar with aquatic fowl as well. Wish I could say this was one of those, but it wasn't. I could easily accept an out-of-place bird if that was the case, and that was something we thought about at the time, but we watched it long enough to know that it didn't fit the bill (pun intended). . . .

"Trust me, this was no water fowl. I have spent many years in Florida, where there are large numbers of those, and this was different. The behavior was all wrong as well. Whatever it was, it was no bird. No crane, stork, pelican, heron, owl, buzzard, eagle, hawk, or any other that I have seen, looked like this. A bat is possible, except that even the *flying fox* (have seen these) isn't anywhere near the size of this thing."

DF then told me about her online posting of her experience and I compared the two reports (she had sent me) to what she had posted on a "sightings" page on cryptozoology.com; I found mostly similar descriptions. She and her brother were adults at the time of the sighting. She allowed for the possibility that the creature's wingspan may have been as little as six feet, but she said, ". . . I believe it was more like 8-10 feet . . ." I was interested in the creature's behavior, for she also said, "This thing flew, or glided, back and forth over the [telephone] wires for at least ten minutes. . . .the flight patterns were wrong." Since bats also fly there, this appeared to confirm an idea I had been pondering for some time: Some *ropens* eat bats.

I remember when that idea first intrigued me. One of my associates had become active in searching for pterosaurs in a secret location (I assumed, at first, in Papua New Guinea). Those who watched the night skies with him were astonished at the light display of large glowing creatures diving and swerving, but most of the flyers were not glowing: They were bats. Astonished I was, on learning the location: in the United States of America.

A few months after my late-2004 expedition in Papua New Guinea, I met Scott Norman. My associate, Garth Guessman, introduced me to this cryptozoologist who had explored in central Africa, searching for the *Mokele-*

mbembe. Scott never saw the *Mokele* dinosaur in Africa, but two years after I met him he became, I believe, the first American cryptozoologist to observe the clear form of a living pterosaur while searching for one.

Scott had doubts about the sightings, in July of 2007, when an investigator talked him into helping them search. (The location is secret, but known to be in the United States.) He planned on visiting an old friend in that state, before taking a turn watching the sky. After he arrived at the search area, he watched a video that investigators had recently recorded: what they thought might be a pterosaur at night. Scott thought it looked like a bird.

Chad Arment reports that Scott said, "[I was] very skeptical and didn't think we would see anything. . . I stayed up till 4:00 a.m. Here's the kicker, the skeptic, between 1:30-2:30 a.m., has a sighting! . . . I was sitting in a chair, sideways towards the shed, looking up at the starry skies, when this animal came gliding just over the shed and into the field . . ."

[From Scott's description of the shed and the flight path, the closest it came to him was probably 20-40 feet.]

The creature's wingspan was roughly nine feet. Scott described the wings: bat-like, because of a "wavy" appearance. He felt that the body could have been over five feet long, with the neck at least a foot long, and the head about four feet. The head crest was about two feet long; it reminded him of that of a *pteranodon* . . . (Others verified Scott reported similar details.)

He saw the creature silhouetted against the stars of the sky; no color was visible. Lack of any sign of a tail interested me, for just a few years earlier a local man had seen, in daylight, what investigators assume was the local pterosaur; it had a tail. Maybe Scott missed the tail in the dark.

Scott wished that the creature had been glowing when it flew over the shed, confirming the concept of large bioluminescent flying creatures. He felt confident that the wingspan was eight to ten feet. He was a bit perplexed that legs were not visible, but like other eyewitnesses of large flying creatures he was concentrating on one or two parts of the cryptid: Apparently Scott was concentrating on the creature's head.

Investigators originally became interested in this area partly because of the flashing lights that suggested *ropens*. But there were also a few reports of daylight sightings: creatures described like pterosaurs. The work still continues here, although I've not yet been invited to participate.

I concluded that Scott saw a living pterosaur rather than a bird or bat (even though many bats fly in this area). Certain aspects of his report indicate that he was telling the truth and had not been dreaming.

A few months after Scott's sighting, he fell ill and, to the sorrow of those who knew him, passed away on February 29, 2008. He is deeply missed in the cryptozoology community.

Cryptozoology author Loren Coleman said, "Scott was a cryptozoologist who had taken his passion for dinosaurs, Mokele-mbembe, and prehistoric cyptids, all the way to Africa. He . . . will be missed . . . In February, 2001, in a joint venture between CryptoSafari and the British Columbia Scientific Cryptozoology Club (B.C.S.C.C.), Scott Norman became a member of a research team, which traveled to the Republic of Cameroon in central-western Africa to investigate . . . Mokele-mbembe sightings."

The pterosaur investigation, by my associates, in the secret location in the United States, drew my attention to the idea that some pterosaurs eat bats, and Scott's death brought these sightings to the attention of the cryptozoology community, for they had previously been kept secret.

Late in 2008, I received an email from a man (DR) who had seen, with his friend, about six years earlier, two pterosaur-like creatures in Florida, also at night. Sitting outside DR's house, in the early morning hours (they had not been drinking or using drugs), the two men saw a creature fly over the roof of the house, toward the backyard. A "long pointed thing protruding from the back of its head," made visible by a flood light illuminating the underside of the creature, as it moved its head to look at them—that is what prompted DR to think it was a pterosaur.

He had lived long enough in Florida to know the common birds; he told me, "I've seen my share of cranes . . . but this was NOT a bird." It had no feathers, but a pointed beak and pointed wing tips, with an estimated wingspan of about four feet. DR, in his email, said something that interested me: "It was a lot smaller than I would think a pterodactyl would be."

The two men had no time to recover when a second creature flew in the opposite direction, toward the neighbor's backyard. (I failed to ask DR how they determined it was not the same creature changing directions.) This one was not as clearly visible, but obviously very similar. DR said to his friend, "Was that what I think it was?" He replied, "Naa, it had to be something else."

DR again emphasized to me that the creatures were not birds. He was convinced that they were either "real pterodactyls" or holographic images of them, and told me, "We BOTH saw the same thing at the same time."

I began questioning DR by email.

Q: Thank you for telling me about your sighting that you experienced around 2002 or 2003. . . . How long was the tail?

A: The tail was about 1' [one foot] long.

Q: Were the two creatures flying in single file? That is, was the second one flying along the same flight path as the first one?

A: . . . the second one went in a complete opposite direction, flying into the backyard of the house directly across the street from us.

Q: How old were you?

A: I was around 25-26 years old.

Q: How long was the head crest or object at the back of the head?

A: The head "thing" was about 3" [three inches] long.

The eyewitness added, ". . . after the sighting . . . we were astonished about what we saw and didn't even talk about it. Before this sighting, I only read about the incident of sewer workers (or miners, I don't remember) where a live perosaur (sic) fell out of some ancient rock . . . when I started to use the internet, I started to research more on the subject, trying to [find] out what me and my friend saw . . . the sighting took place when I lived in Jupiter, Florida." (end of interview)

Earlier in 2008, a man tried to reach me by telephone. After he left me a phone message, we communicated by email about his daylight sighting, which was not years but just hours earlier.

"Hi, my name is [MR] and I live at . . . Bowling Green, Kentucky. Today I opened my back door around 4:30 p.m. to smoke a cigarette and I noticed a large bird in the sky flying above me. I thought it seemed strange because I [saw] a tail with a spade-like end; also the wingspan was a lot larger than any bird I have ever seen around here. The wings did not flutter rapidly: Each wing stroke was steady and powerful. The bird seemed to have a set destination . . . 'cause it did not waste any time moving through the sky.

"I thought about running in to grab my camera but I knew that by the way it was flying that it would have been gone before I got back, so I watched in awe as this bird streaked [across] the sky to the southeast of where I live. I am positive 100% about the tail, there [were] overcast [skies] today, so the sun was not glaring in my eyes. Anyways, I hope that this information is helpful in some way. I'll keep my camera nearby and will continue to look for what I [have] seen today.

"I am confident [that] what I [saw] was absolutely not a standard bird with feathers; there were no feathers that I could see. I was so transfixed on the tail of this creature that I did not notice the head."

Q: About how close was the closest the creature came to you?

A: I can't say for certain how close it was from me because when I noticed it was there, it was already passing above me. The creature made a slight curve in its flight from south to a li'l more east but still remaining [in] the S.E. position. . . . I am aware that judging [the size of] an object in the air without some kind of background such as trees or lightpoles is almost impossible. All I can say is the bird was large enough for me to notice it flying above me and strange enough for me to remember for the rest of my life. I have been trying to find out all I can, after this happened. Do you get many reports on these type of descriptions? The bird was flying way higher than the other birds were.

Q: I receive reports like this from many parts of the world. For about how many seconds did you see this creature?

A: It was around 60 seconds.

I then telephoned MR and questioned him along somewhat similar lines. I was impressed with his credibility. What he said and how he responded to my questioning gave me confidence in his honesty.

I had suspected that sixty seconds was an overestimate of the length of the sighting. From details in our phone conversation, I estimated it was probably closer to forty-five seconds. The creature's course began towards the southeast but then shifted slightly: more east than south.

MR is not from Kentucky, so someone else at his house told him about the heading: approximately towards Russellville (but this is west-by-southwest of Bowling Green); MR reaffirmed, however, that the direction was southeast. It seems that the nearest body of water is about two miles away, southeast of the sighting location. There is also a branch of Drakes Creek in that general direction. Water seems important for long-tailed *ropens*.

In 2007, I received an email from a young lady in Richmond, Virginia.

"My father has been the subject of much ridicule after claiming to have seen a "dinosaur bird" fly across the moon. His neighbor has a telescope and they'd been watching the sky when they saw it. My sister and I dismissed it, although I couldn't think of anything he could have seen and mistook for a "dinosaur bird." My father later told me that he'd done some research and learned that they were called "ropen." I went online, and to my surprise, Dad wasn't making it up. I just wanted to go on record as saying that they've been sighted from here in Richmond." [AS]

Later I received an email from a man in Wisconsin.

" . . . wanted to tell someone about a sighting I had back in the late 1970's or early 1980's. I grew up on a farm and picked cucumbers to make money as a kid. All of my sisters and brother did also. Anyways one late afternoon, I had just brought out the tractor to pick up the bags of cucumbers when I noticed a strange looking bird in the sky. Unfortunately I was the only one out there at the time. The thing that caught my eye was that it looked like something straight out of the dinosaurs era. It scared the . . . out of me right away. I knew it was not a sand hill crane, which we have a few hundred migrating thru. What stood out was the long pointed head and the fact that there was a very long tail between the legs and with a ball shaped on the end of it. It flew from the north going south and turned around and then went back north. I knew that there was a large marsh up north about a mile or so and thought it might have come from there. I will remember this sighting forever. Well take care" [EWED]

Also in 2007, I received an email from a man who saw something unusual at the end of a flying creature's tail.

"I feel like I should report this just in case someone else sees this animal. I was driving from Muskegon, Michigan, to Fremont, at 8 p.m., with my family, on 8-18-07 [only hours earlier than this email]. It was still light out but it was raining gently and cloudy. I was on US-31, going north, in fairly heavy traffic, just leaving the city before Highway M-120, when in the sky just above and in front of our car, I saw a large dark colored bird flying from the west (Lake Michigan area) to the east, into the woods. At first glance, it didn't look extraordinary; it looked like a [heron] or crane bird. After looking at it more thoroughly, I saw that it had a spike out the back of the head. Then I saw a long tail with a diamond shape at its end. It seemed to be of dark color Brown or black. The animal was seen very clearly and the tail and diamond shaped end was also unmistakably clear." [RT]

It's common for an eyewitness to first assume that what is seen is a bird. In Kentucky, MR first assumed he was watching a "large bird." In Wisconsin, EWED first assumed a "strange looking bird." In Michigan, RT first assumed an ordinary "large dark colored bird." This refutes one explanation offered, by our critics, against the concept of living pterosaurs.

Over several years, I have encountered several explanations for accounts of living pterosaurs. Do my associates and I, who've searched for *ropens*, really "see what we want to see?" Obviously not literally, considering the years of expeditions in Papua New Guinea, years of searching for living pterosaurs while we observed nothing clearly resembling one. No, our critics believe that our bias causes us to interpret evidence wrongly, that we see what we want to see in the sense of misinterpreting data.

But it is the eyewitnesses who see apparent living pterosaurs, and many of them, when they first noticed something flying, assumed "a bird." The point? Eyewitnesses are not biased in favor of living pterosaurs, yet details of appearance caused them to conclude that they had seen pterosaurs: the diamond-shaped end-of-tail, or featherless-creature-with-headcrest. Nobody "wants to see" these pterosaur-features on what is first assumed to be a bird. The explanation? Maybe they really did see living pterosaurs.

Soon after returning from my expedition in Papua New Guinea, I received an email from SLR. The description of the "pterodactyle" was welcome, although, after my questioning, not precisely "what I wanted to see."

" . . . It was probably 1982 when me and my older brother were sitting in our carport at Union Village Apartments, in Texarkana, AR. It was getting dark but there was plenty of light in the sky when we saw what we believe to be a pterodactyle. The wingspan seemed to be about 25' to 30' ft wide. It was probably about 70' to 80' off the ground, flying over a large tree in front of the house. I never saw the wings flap; it just glided on air. The incident was very brief but nonetheless was an awesome sight to see. If someone would have told me that they had seen a creature like that, I doubt I would have believed the story until I saw it for myself. Well, needless to say, I believe and am always on the lookout. I hope that investigations will continue. I do believe eventually one of these creatures will be captured or found right here in the USA." [SLR]

I thanked the eyewitness and began the email interview.

Q: For how many seconds (or minutes) did you see it?

A: We saw the creature for approximately 20 seconds.

Q: Was there any sign of feathers or any sign of fur or was it leathery or naked skin?

A: We did not see any signs of feathers, just sharp edged wings, the sharp pointed beak, and the sharp pointed crest on its head.

Q: Did it have any tail? [long-tailed flying cryptids are my specialty]

A: We did not see any tail. I have looked at my dinosaur book and the picture of the pteranodon looked like what we saw. [end of interview]

Most sighting reports that I've received, from around the world, involve a flying creature with a tail. This sighting in Texarkana was an exception, but a significant minority of reports are of tail-less creatures.

About three years later (about 1985), and 420 miles to the northwest, in Woodward, Oklahoma, near a small river, at about noon, a fourteen-year-old became terrified at the sight of a pterosaur-like creature.

"I was walking to the small river where I usually caught carp fish. . . . a large animal took off into the air. At first I thought it was an eagle. Then I noticed it was a dinosaur. I went to my knees so that it would not see me. I was afraid it would eat me. I stared at the back part of the head because it was exactly like the ones depicted in books. . . . had a long neck and wide wings just like in the movies or in books. It had no feathers and it was flying around and looking downwards into the fields. I guess it was looking for food. I was really afraid. As it started to fly away, I still waited until I could not see it . . . [so I could safely] go back home. I never told anyone about this until now. People think you're crazy when you tell them about something like this. The creature [looked] like it was dark brown. I was really close to it. About the feet or tail, I cannot remember either, but I believe it had feet and a tail." [BB]

Of course that fourteen-year-old boy did not see "what he wanted to see." Some critics suggest that fear causes eyewitnesses to misidentify what was seen, that common birds or bats have been observed instead of pterosaurs. Well, let us consider that: When was the last time you were terrified at the sight of a common bird? Consider details in these reports. The uncommon appearance causes fear, especially when it's the last thing ones wants to see. In harmony with that, the principle is not nullified by this boy's age.

At about the same time as the Texarkana sighting, between Houston and Pasadena, Texas, two men saw a pterosaur-like creature, but it was smaller and with a tail. I've not yet interviewed either eyewitness; my associate, the cryptozoologist Ken Gerhard (*Big Bird* book author), has.

RG and his friend, in the late afternoon of a clear day, were startled by a flying creature less than 150 feet away. For about fifteen seconds, they watched it fly, about fifty feet high, before it disappeared into some trees. The general appearance was "leathery" and it had a pointed beak and head appendage. The total length, about five feet, included about two feet of tail, the end of which had a "flange or sail."

Before his interview with Gerhard, RG was ridiculed by those who heard his story. I feel for eyewitnesses who are the victims of cultural bias; but I'm grateful for this man's report. I hope he no longer feels alone.

Aaron Tullock was eight years old (about 1995) when he saw a hovering flying creature, most uncommon. Late in a sunny afternoon in Marion County, Texas, he was alone in the yard of his grandparent's house.

"I saw a featherless flying animal with a wingspan of about $4^{1}/_{2}$ to 5 feet and a long tail with a diamond type shape at the tip of it. No hair or feathers anywhere, just leathery reptile type skin. I have a well established knowledge of animals, especially reptiles, so I can easily tell what animal something is and what it isn't. The animal had bumps down its back, feet with longish toes, and long black claws like an osprey has for grasping fish . . . a long mouth/beak full of long sharp teeth that somewhat protruded from the mouth like a crocodiles [mouth] when closed.

"Its color was bright orange with black 'tiger stripes,' far brighter and more noticeable than you would think an unknown animal would be but that's what I saw. . . . although the animal was brightly colored, the underside was not brightly colored; it was more of a cream color, like dirty clouds . . . The colorless underside may be a type of camouflage . . . Just a personal theory. Anything else, please ask me . . . contact me anytime."

Mr. Tullock has reported his sighting to one or two other cryptozoologists (it might be published elsewhere), so I will only summarize it.

This rural area is two counties south of Texarkana, Texas. The creature flew from an area of forest and thick swamp and stopped while hovering about eight feet off the ground, near the grandparents' house. The boy noticed that the wings were beating louder when hovering than when it had been flying overhead; nevertheless, the wing beats were relatively quiet. Mr. Tullock told me, "If I wanted to I could have jumped and grabbed its tail, but that probably would have gone wrong."

Nothing obstructed the boy's view of the creature. He told me, "I was quite awe struck by the animal's being there and me seeing it, since it was so out of place." He was well aware of standard teachings about extinction.

"It had a tail about 3 feet long with the characteristic flange on the end; it had no head crest and no feathers at all, although there was kind of a longish bump on the back of the head . . . It faced away from me most of the time . . . [The] long pointy teeth [were] about $1^1/_2$ inches . . .

"I only remember one or two claws on each wing, still fuzzy on that because it's been so long. . . . The flange on its tail had a small diamond shape in the center with 'veins' going out from it. . . ."

After about a minute or two, Tullock watched it ascend up to about fifty feet and then fly away. When his mother came out of the house, he told her that he had seen a pterodactyl; she dismissed it as a bird and his imagination, but I'm grateful that he eventually reported his experience to me.

I'm also grateful to have received a report from a young lady who was a child when she had a sighting in Brownsville, Texas. I'll call her "GR."

She was twelve years old, at most (around 1995), when she walked out into her backyard one morning to check on the dog, for the dog food was untouched. GR found the poor animal cowering around the side of the house, apparently trying to hide behind a banana tree. The girl had no idea what was wrong, at that time, and called the dog, but it would not move. Fearing it was sick, GR was about to run back into the house to tell her mother. A weird noise made her stop. She turned her head and saw what it was that had terrified the dog.

Next door, in the neighbor's backyard, was what she first thought was a tall man; but he was about as tall as the house, too tall. He was "draped in a long black coat or cape," facing away from her. "Dracula" came to mind as GR tried to understand what she was looking at. The "man" turned, and revealed a face that terrified the child: It was non-human.

Slowing the creature (revealing itself to be neither human nor bird) unwrapped its bat-like wings, dark leathery wings. The girl had never seen anything remotely like them. Her mind still raced for an explanation, something that would make sense of what see was watching. A large bird, maybe? No, it was nothing like that: too big, and without feathers. The girl was frozen in fear, watching what the thing would do.

With big black eyes, it stared at her, and began to walk towards her. Now the idea of "large bird" was gone, leaving in its place fear of the unknown. Distracted by some noise, fortunately, the creature turned away from the girl, revealing to her another perspective of its head. "Pterodactyl" came into her mind, although it seemed a crazy idea.

Unfortunately, the creature turned back towards the girl. She slowly crept backwards towards the back door, hoping to get inside in time. The creature then gently lifted up off the ground, floating or gliding at her, but the girl just managed to dive through the door, slamming it behind her.

She tried to explain what had happened, crying hysterically, but she was the only eyewitness; her little sister had seen only the passing shadow through the window. Her efforts to convince others of her experience all failed. Blue heron photos were shown to her, for naught. She knew that what she had encountered was nothing like any picture of any bird her father could show her. Ridicule followed, but she knew that she had seen a "pterodactyl," and nobody could convince her otherwise.

In her email to me, she described something I found interesting: "a stump looking thing on the top of its head that was kind of long." The beak was slanted a bit, long and pointed. The wingspan she estimated at about thirty feet. How easy to understand her fear! [End of report by GR]

I found her account convincing, with nothing to suggest any perception problem or dishonesty. This eyewitness account needs our serious consideration, for the giant creature she described was neither bird nor bat.

A sighting in Missouri was reported to me by a researcher asking advice on how to interview the eyewitness. I suggested questions, he added some of his own; I was thus only indirectly involved with interviewing BG. We are indebted to this new researcher, Peter Theiss; thank you, Peter.

The man and his grandmother saw the large apparently smooth-skinned creature, on July 15, 2004, flying about a hundred feet above an Arby's restaurant in St. Louis.

Q: Did you catch sight of the head?

A: Yes, it did not have the long crest on top; the creature's head and body was very similar like Rhamphorhynchus.

Q: Did its wings have claws on them?

A: I couldn't tell, it wasn't close enough to distinguish that, but it did have the diamond-shaped tail end.

Q: For how many seconds (or minutes) was the sighting?

A: . . . about 30 seconds

Q: What time of day or night?

A: . . . between 7:00 and 7:30 pm, it was still good daylight at the time.

Q: Was anyone else with you during the sighting?

A: Yes, I was with my grandmother, and she saw it too and she also said that it was a pterosaur.

Q: Is the area . . . rural?

A: No . . . this was a busy street with lots of traffic . . . I didn't see anyone else, other than my grandmother, notice the creature.

Q: Were any legs visible?

A: The animal [was] high up and we couldn't see much over its underside but I'm sure it did have legs.

Q: How wide would you estimate its wings were?

A: [It's] hard to be precise, but I say around twenty feet; it could have been a bit wider though . . . an impressive wingspan . . . widest I've ever seen.

Q: How long was it from its "beak" to the end of its tail?

A: Again, it's difficult to be precise, it was quite long at maybe 10 feet; its tail was several feet itself so it's indeed possible it could have been even longer than I said.

Q: What color was it?

A: It was light tannish color, I couldn't see any distinctive markings . . .

Q: Did you ever [see] any other dinosaur-like creatures?

A: No, except for birds [BG believes birds evolved from dinosaurs.]

Q: Was the diamond-shaped tail end hairy?

A: . . . I couldn't see any details like that . . .

BG could not be sure that the creature had no feathers but he was impressed (but less than 100% sure) that it had smooth skin. Several points impressed me with the credibility of this eyewitness, although I was hardly involved with the interview. I believe he was telling the truth, with very low probability of having misidentified a bird or bat.

Another researcher received an email from a lady in Rhode Island. I was grateful that she responded to my email. She reported a "pterodactyl," (October, 2001, sighting) with a "width" of about fifteen feet. PB became scared after the creature had circled her house a few times.

PB emailed me: "Yes I will be happy to answer your questionnaire. . . . I have only mentioned this to a few people. The [animal] had two small claw-like feet on the underside that looked like they would be useless."

A day earlier, she had sent me an email with a general account of what she had experienced: ". . . I heard a loud whooshing noise moving in the air to my right. I saw a huge pterodactyl. It circled my house six times and once it turned its head and looked at me. By the sixth time, it was somewhat lower; it definitely was interested in me. I am not a nut; I'm a mother of two and work in a hospital . . . I can't believe more people don't report seeing them." Later she told me that she found me through web "surfing."

PB also mentioned, "I got a good look at it, and by the last time it flew by I was scared. I backed up against the side of the house close to my sliding glass door . . . This is something that people don't talk about too much. The day after I saw it I listened to the radio, read the paper waiting for someone to report seeing it too, but days and weeks went by, and nothing. I think there must be more people like me that have seen them, but are reluctant to report what they saw. I hope you see one and get it on film . . ." [This was only a few weeks before my expedition on Umboi Island, Papua New Guinea.] She continued, "They are hunters, the one I saw circled my house because it saw me, I saw it physically turn its head to get a better look. I don't think I told you, but there was a huge whooshing noise when it was approaching. . . . it was about 25 feet in the air." [end of PB interview]

Also in 2001, but in Camden, Maine, a creature with "leathery" wings was reported to have flown over a residential neighborhood. The wingspan was estimated at twenty-four feet, but this estimate was not from a wild guess: The creature flew just above the roof of a house. [eyewitness SF]

Also in the Northeast (east of Buffalo, New York), a "pterodactyl" was seen. I received this email in mid-2007, just weeks after the sighting:

" . . . my friend and I were canoeing in the creek accessed from my back yard, when we sighted a very strange creature that we had both thought to be a prehistoric bird. Immediately, I thought 'pterodactyl.' It was a greyish color with no apparent feathers. I remember the wing span and the head shape but I don't recall the tail end.

"It was only visible for a few moments before it disappeared into the tree line. It coasted in movement; I don't recall the wings flapping. It was off into the distance, so size is difficult to determine. I would estimate the wing span to be six feet. It was the most bizarre thing I ever saw. We were looking after, to see if it had perched, as we were paddling up the creek, but did not see it again. . . . I know that I saw this creature. I wish I would of had a camera; I will from now on."

I replied to DC:

Q: How many people saw the creature at that time?

A: There were two of us paddling a canoe . . . I saw it first. My friend just saw it for an instant, but doesn't recall any detail except for its large size.

Q: Are you familiar with the birds in this area?

A: No, not really familiar, until I looked up large birds on the internet, and I have since seen a Blue Heron, which was not what I saw. It was much smaller and different in color.

Q: When you mentioned "wing span," did you mean the length from one wingtip to the other wingtip? Or did you mean the size of only one wing?

A: From one wingtip to the other wingtip.

Q: In regard to how it was flying, can you classify it . . . [flight direction]

A: Flying right but getting a little further away.

DC then put me on the spot: "I have a question for you if I may. Have you ever seen one?"

I answered, "I have never seen a *ropen* or anything . . . related to it. I have spent two weeks on Umboi Island, looking for the giant *ropen* there; I had to leave the hill-top camp after a problem arose with local villagers. Later, near another village, I went to sleep one hour before my interpreter and a village leader saw the *ropen* flying near Mount Bel."

I continued, "Most people who have seen these creatures have just been fortunate to have been at the right place, at the right time, looking in the right direction. You were one of the lucky ones. . . ." [end of interview]

Also in 2007, I received a report of another daylight sighting (by DP). To understand his use of the word "pterodactyl," we need to remember that most Americans use it as a general term for "pterosaur." The technically correct usage is for a specific species. But DP seems to be using the word for "Pterodactyloid," which is a group of pterosaurs that is distinct from the *Rhamphorhynchoid* group, at least in one old classification system.

"My wife and I both read your book, *Searching for Ropens*, and enjoyed it very much. I was interested in your book and purchased it because of an unusual experience I had back in 1990 which I would like to share . . ."

"Some of the details (date, place, time, etc) I do not remember exactly, but what I saw I remember distinctly and will never forget. I was twenty years old, taking a camping trip with my boss and his friends, and I believe it was near the Maryland-Virginia line in the Chesapeake area. We were tubing [inner-tube] in the river, some time in the morning or early afternoon. It was a very serene environment, trees on both sides for a few miles.

"My boss and I suddenly saw, parallel with the water, quite a distance away, a flying object that was strange. Why? Because we knew it was quite far away, but it was as big as a regular bird would appear up close. It was gliding, with an occasional slow, smooth flap. We were talking about it, but, as it approached, words ceased, and amazement took over. It flew directly over us, about twenty yards above us, and as I turned my inner tube along its path, it perched on a tree about fifty yards past us. A minute later, it flew away along the same river path, and I've never seen anything like it since.

"I know what it was. It wasn't a heron; it wasn't a vulture; it wasn't an albatross. I had spent countless hours as a child studying dinosaurs and playing with dinosaur models. I know what I saw.

"There was one peculiar difference from my knowledge of pterodactyls [read Pterodactyloids] and rhamphorhynchoids. I had always learned that pterodactyls have the protruded head [head crest], with a stubby tail, if any, while rhamphorhynchoids had the long tail with a diamond tip. This one, however, had a pterodactyl protruded head and a rhamphorhynchoid diamond-tipped tail. I believe you call it a rhamphorhynchoid-pterosaur [actually, when descriptions suggest a *Rhamphorhynchoid* pterosaur, I usually call it "ropen"] I've seen it. It's hard to be exact about the size. . . . wing-tip to wing-tip, about 12+ feet? I don't even know if I'm close. And the length, I'd estimate about 10 feet? It was brown and leathery.

"After the encounter, oddly, no one felt comfortable speaking about it except me. My boss acknowledged the sighting but seemed uneasy for some reason about pursuing any conversation about it. I haven't told many people because I did not think they would believe me. I've searched in books about birds but have never found anything remotely like what I saw that day. When I saw your web site and read your book, I was excited to realize that other people had seen and believed in the existence of such a creature. I thought you would be interested in my experience. I also wondered whether any research [had] been done on sightings in this country."

"Thank you for an enjoyable book [*Searching for Ropens*]. Please let me know if you have any questions about what I saw. . . . I am a high school theology/philosophy teacher with a master's degree in theology, and I appreciate the motivation behind your research."

I replied to DP, "Thank you . . . Over several years, I have received many sighting reports of creatures in the United States. . . . What you describe is not unusual to me, though it is either shocking or unbelievable to most Americans; that's because of our cultural environment . . . What you describe has been seen in various states . . . May I ask some questions?

Q: Have you communicated with any other person who has seen anything at all like what you saw?

A: No, I haven't . . .

Q: Was the weather hot, warm, cool, or cold?

A: . . mid to late summer, noon time, give or take a couple hours . . . hot

Q: . . . the wingspan may have been a bit greater than the length . . . (?)

A: The approximate measurements are very difficult to estimate. Although I estimated the wingspan at 12 ft and the length at 10 ft, it could be the other way around. [end of interview with DP]

At about the same time, a lady [BEW] had a daylight encounter northwest of Wichita. In early 2006, she found my web site and contacted me.

"My friend and I were talking and I mentioned that I had seen an extremely large bird that resembled a pterodactyl some years ago when [I was] driving to town from the family farm between Rush Center and Larned, Kansas. I could not believe my eyes as I immediately thought of a prehistoric bird when I saw it. It must have had a wing-span of 16-20 feet.

"I asked my friend what kind of bird it could have been. We looked at pictures on the internet to see if we could figure anything out. I know he thought I had a vivid imagination, etc. So I decided to check further and ran across this site. I was amazed to find a lot written about others who claim to have seen such a bird. I never said too much to anyone about it because, of course, such a claim raises eyebrows. Also, I figured if I saw it others must have too (you couldn't miss it); but I never heard anything about it from anyone else."

I replied, "Thank you . . . May I ask some questions about your sighting? I appreciate the difficulty many people have in reporting something that resembles a pterosaur. I promise to treat your report with an open mind. You are not alone."

From BEW: "Please feel free to ask me any questions. It's been probably 15-16 years since I saw the bird."

Q: How far was the bird or creature from you when you watched it?

A: I would say 60-100 feet up at the closest.

Q: Could you tell if it had feathers?

A: It did not appear to have feathers.

Q: Are you familiar with the larger birds in Kansas?

A: Somewhat

Q: How was this thing different from larger birds you know of?

A: I've never seen any bird in Kansas a fraction of that size or with the appearance of this bird.

Q: What was it doing when you saw it?

A: Soaring slowly towards the northeast.

Q: What was the time of year and time of day?

A: I don't recall exactly. It was warm and about early afternoon.

She included, "This bird looked textbook pterodactyl. I am curious if any other Kansans have reported such a sighting? The bird took my breath away. I have not been obsessed about this but it came up in conversation and revived my curiosity. Can you tell me of any other birds of Kansas that would match the description?"

I replied, "This is interesting . . . There are some possibly similar reports from the Midwest, but I want to be careful and not jump to a conclusion just yet. May we continue with questions and answers?"

During an interview, I don't want to give an eyewitness a false sense of my understanding of these creatures. My associates and I are not close to understanding modern pterosaur species, but we know of two general types: long-tailed and those without long tails. We have assumed that the descriptions refer to *Rhamphorhynchoids* and *Pterodactyloids*; but we still live within the confines of cryptozoology, not zoology. We still need to remember that capturing living creatures, or finding their remains, will allow detailed examination and eventual classification. But I usually give the eyewitnesses no more than a brief explanation during an interview.

I continued questioning BEW about the sighting northwest of Wichita.

Q: How high was it above the ground?

A: I would estimate the closest from the ground it got was 60-100 feet. I'm not real familiar with estimations like this, because not often have I had to guesstimate distance upwards.

Q: How was it situated in terms of direction, in other words, was it north of you or south, west, east, or northwest, etc?

A: It was nearly straight above me when I first saw it. I don't recall what made me look up. I say this because it was not at much of an angle at all when I first saw it.

Q: What direction was it flying in relation to you . . . ? [This set of questions, beginning with "How high," were sent as a group, in an email, so questions may appear odd, at times, in relation to the answers, which also come in a group. This is typical of email interviews.]

A: It appeared to be headed to the north/northeast. I got a very good view of it from all sides. At first I stared in awe at it, of course, because it left me gasping at what I might be seeing. The thing that sticks out in my mind is that I got a very prolonged view of it. I don't remember exactly why that was, though. I faintly remember it soaring around.

Q: Did you get a good look at the head? What was it like?

A: The head was very distinctive. It looked like what might [be] described as a hammer-head.

Q: Did it have a tail? If so, how long was the tail, compared with the distance from wing-tip to wing-tip?

A: It may have had a tail, but the feet kind of hung behind.

Q: When you mentioned the "wingspan" being 16-20 feet, I assume this is the distance from one wing-tip to the other wing-tip. Is that right?

A: I would say that was tip-to-tip.

She continued, "Really the wings and the head were what mostly caught my attention and the way it was moving."

Q: Did you notice any color to the creature?

A: I do not recall any color. . . . I am recalling . . . a light shade of grey.

Q: Is there any large body of water near this place?

A: There are some large man-made lakes (3 or 4) within a hundred miles from here. There are several ponds and creeks locally. . . . when I saw it, I distinctly remember thinking that I wished I hadn't because there was no one around to corroborate with me. It seems so very odd that no one else reported this around here; but I know without a doubt what I saw was huge and looked like I described it. Thanks for taking time to hear me. [BEW]

I've read many sighting reports online, including the internet pages of cryptozoology.com. A posting in 2006 caught my attention, resulting in my interviewing two boys who describe an apparent *Rhamphorhynchoid* pterosaur flying in Zionsville, Indiana. Although two circumstances do suggest, slightly, the possibility of a hoax, those two points are overshadowed by evidences against a hoax; I believe the two boys were telling the truth. (Details related to hoax potential, in testimonies, I still keep secret, to avoid unwittingly contributing to any future hoax; thus, if a person tries a hoax, the falsity will be easier to expose.)

Through the living-room window, IM noticed a "flying creature" strange in shape: small body, triangular wings, no feathers. The body he described as the shape of an "elongated-lemon." The long straight tail had "a swelling at the end shaped, again, somewhat like a lemon." With rapid wing-flapping, the small creature flew away. The boy called his friend, who also had seen the creature fly near his own house. IM concluded, "We believe we have reason to believe this is a Rhamphorhynchus, a small primitive pterosaur of the Jurassic period."

Additional comments from IM, along with his answers to my questions, diminished the possibility of a hoax. He wrote: "I would be delighted to be interviewed . . . I'm glad somebody is interested in my sighting."

Q: About what time was it when you first saw the creature?

A: I first saw the potential pterasaur (sic) at about [5:20 p.m.]

Q: How fast was it flying? Can you imagine a car driving through your neighborhood with this creature flying next to the car? (I assume that cars around your house drive at about 25 m.p.h.) Would the car be faster or slower than the creature?

A: I assume, in the general speed of cars in front of my house, that the thing was flying a bit slower than your presumption of a car's speed. It seemed to be flitting its wings around like a bat, but more to stay aloft than for speed. It moved at a fairly fast gliding speed.

Q: What color was the creature?

A: The day was a cloudy day where everything seems darker than it is. The pterasaur (sic) seemed to my eyes to be black, and the pine trees below it seemed a mix of green and gray, so [I] assume the creature was a darkish color a few degrees below black.

Q: Was it at all similar in color to any bird that you know?

A: The color would probably have been similar to any bird you would see flying on that day because of the poor lighting. However, the shape was similar to a great blue heron, except for several bodily differences.

Q: Is it possible that there were feathers on the creature?

A: [It] is possible that there were feathers on the creature, but the thing was the size of a small hawk, and most hawks have observable primary flight feathers. [I] observed no flight feathers and no tail feathers above what would have been the legs in a great blue heron.

Q: Was the head a different color than the body?

A: Sorry about the scanty information, but I did not see the head, though I saw the whole rest of the body. It must have been tucked under the body.

Q: Did you tell anybody about this right away? (If so, who?)

A: Yes, I told one of my best friends, [IA], about the Rhamphorynchus (sic) right away. I was surprised when he informed me he had also just seen it heading for my neighborhood!

How burdened is the lone eyewitness who sees a living pterosaur! How common, when more than one sees a living pterosaur, for only one of them to talk about it! But in Zionsville, Indiana, two boys seem to have seen a *Rhamphorhynchoid* pterosaur, and then talked about it. (The identities of most eyewitnesses I keep secret, including those of these two boys.)

The second boy, IA, remembers that the sighting was on a weekend. He was about to take a walk, when he noticed something through the window of his brother's bedroom. What he first assumed to be a bird flew close to the window, revealing its color: a "deep scarlet." Also, "Its face was very angular and almost eerie to view." Because it flew fast and close to the window, little else was noticed at first. Then the creature landed in the street, revealing a pigeon-size, but no pigeon-resemblance.

I made a brief analysis of the credibility of these two boys and found at least a four-to-one ratio of positive-to-negative points in their favor. They were probably telling the truth.

One year before interviewing the boys, I interviewed a young man who reported a long-tailed flying creature 117 miles to the northeast, on a hot summer day in Antwerp, Ohio. As with the Zionsville sightings, I was not able to completely eliminate a non-pterosaur explanation; nevertheless, our interviews caused me to believe that he probably saw a pterosaur. I refer to this young man as "ZJ."

"It was huge. . . . About 4.5 ft tall, 10 ft from head to end of tail. Long skinny tail with a spade about 3-4 [inches] from end of tail. It had a wing span of I would say 8-10 ft. Dark green skin sort of like an alligator. It had round long pointed teeth, jutting out in every direction and [its] snout was long and skinny.

"I seen it catching sparrows that were catching bugs off the top of the river. I was driving across a bridge out to my friend's house, when the damn thing nearly ran into the side of my car. They fly so incredibly graceful. So much more than any kind of bird. Well anyway, it effortlessly flew over my car and that is when I stopped (in fear of having it hit my side window) and got out of my car to see it fly over the other side of the bridge. That is when I seen it swoop lower and start catching those sparrows. I think these [long-tailed creatures] are migratory, I've seen this thing on another occasion the following summer. It comes here regularly."

Q: Thank you . . . Where was your sighting?

A: [ZJ replied] My sighting was just outside Antwerp, OH. On a bridge that crosses the Maumee River.

Q: If I understand, you've seen this creature more than once, right? Do you know what the dates were [?] . . .

A: Yes I have seen this more than once, I seen it 07/2002 and around the same time in 2003.

Q: . . . Is this the bridge that Route 49 takes over this river?

A: yes . . . that very same bridge.

Q: . . . have [you] seen more than one at a time?

A: No . . .

Q: Did you ever see this creature standing?

A: No I haven't, only in flight.

Q: Did you see it catch a sparrow?

A: Yes, I did.

Q: Have you reported these sightings to anyone else besides me? (official or not - friends or anyone at all)

A: Yes I have, but I do not remember who anymore.

Q: Are you sure the creature seen in 2002 was the same type of creature as seen in 2003? (. . . the same type, not the exact same creature . . .)

A: Yes, it was the same creature. . . . it may of even been the same one.

Q: Did you ever get a good look at the head? Was there anything unusual about the head that you could describe?

A: It's (sic) head had a rudder like thing on the back, but apart (sic) of [its] cranium. Also, [its] eyes were completely black, almost as if it had evolved that way to reduce glare. [Its] teeth were round like pens and they were pointed at the tip. They went out in different directions.

Q: Was there anything unusual about the tail?

A: The only thing that stood out on the tail was that it was long and skinny, it also had a spade on it about 3 or 4 inches from the very end [of] it.

Q: Is there a chance it had feathers?

A: Absolutely no feathers . . .

Q: What did you do the first time you saw the creature?

A: I'll admit my heart beat faster, but I wasn't all that scared, just surprised, I was even more excited when I seen it cause I knew exactly what it was, when I seen it.

Q: . . . any other bridges like this . . . over a river like the Maumee . . . ?

A: Yes, Cecil Bridge and Forters Bridge both cross the Maumee . . . going down the river in the same direction.

Q: When you saw it catch the sparrow, did you see how it was done? How did the creature catch the sparrow?

A: When it caught the sparrow it just swooped down and circled back.

Q: What time of day . . . ?

A: About 6:00 pm, around the hottest time of day around here.

Q: May I speak with you by telephone?

A: If you want I suppose, 419- . . .

Q: Do you know anyone else who has seen it?

A: No one else to my knowledge. [end of this email interview]

A telephone interview is most useful in establishing the credibility of an eyewitness. Although not all his answers were what I had hoped for, my phone conversation with ZJ did strengthen his credibility, in my view.

Telephone interview (answers digested and edited by me):

Q: Would you like to be [anonymous]?

A: [doesn't matter]

Q: Did you see the creature in 2002 and in 2003?

A: Yes

Q: When you told somebody about this, was it a friend or . . . not . . . ?

A: Friend

Q: Which year was it that you saw the creature catch the sparrow?

A: 2002 (first time)

Q: Did it catch the sparrow with its feet or mouth?

A: Mouth

Q: Was the sparrow in front of the creature when the sparrow was caught?

(If to the side, which side?)

A: Birds were flying across river while creature was following river. (It seems bird flew into path of creature?)

Q: . . . was the creature flying away from you?

A: Yes

Q: What happened with the tail when the capture took place?

A: (Nothing special noticed.)

Q: Did you see the creature turn in the air once or more than once? (how many times?) How did the tail move when the creature changed directions? Did it ever move the tail up? Did it ever move the tail down? Did it ever twist the tail?

A: The tail was flexible like a cat's tail. At least once, the creature flew over the bridge.

Q: Was the spade near the end of the tail horizontal or vertical or in between?

A: Unsure

Q: How did you find my email address?

A: (looking for someone who had seen what he had seen)

Q: Can you tell me anything about the "rudder like thing" on the back of the head?

A: It was rounded: 1/2 to 3/4 of the length of the mouth.

Q: Have you looked in any books, trying to find out what kind of creature this is? What do you think it is?

A: Pteranodon? [See paragraph at the bottom of this page.]

Q: Do you think it is unusual for people to see this kind of creature in the United States?

A: (ZJ replied that his friend, [LW], who lives in Payne, knows someone who has seen it.)

Q: What are your feelings about this creature?

A: Migratory

Q: Can you tell me anything about yourself?

A: (23 years old; lived most or all of his life in Antwerp, a town with under 2000 residents, but it has a small newspaper, police station, and stores.)

During my five years of interviewing those who describe live pterosaurs, I have found only a few who were obviously either trying to deceive or trying to describe a delusion-or-hallucination. ZJ was not one of them. After reviewing his two interviews, his answers and comments increased my confidence in his honesty and in his mental health. He seems to be a normal eyewitness, reporting what he actually experienced.

It bothered me, at first: his description of tail-movement as flexible, like a cat's tail. Although ZJ offered "pteranodon" as a possible candidate for the creature, his description makes it an obvious *Rhamphorhynchoid* (to me, that is, for the *ropen* of Umboi Island seems to be a giant *Rhamphorhynchoid* with a head crest). But this type of pterosaur, according to fossil evidence (supported by native accounts on Umboi Island), has a tail that is rather stiff, except near where it connects to the body; the *Rhamphorhynchoid* tail is hardly flexible like a cat's tail. On closer examination of his testimony, however, I realized that he did not say that the tail moved like the tail of a cat: He gave his opinion that it had that flexibility. And that opinion may have been influenced by how the creature was flying.

Long-tailed pterosaurs have been reported with stiff tails, except for the report by ZJ. But what's different about the creature seen flying over the Maumee River? Why would this apparent pterosaur seem to have a tail that is flexible? The answer lies in how it was flying: catching sparrows.

When I was a child, I learned a magic trick: bending a pencil without breaking it. Try it yourself. Hold one end of the pencil, using only your thumb and index finger. Keeping the hand steady, wiggle your thumb slightly. When the hand is unmoved, the slight thumb-wiggling moves the pencil, but there's no magic, for the pencil still looks quite straight. Now hold the end of the pencil with only enough strength to keep it from falling out of your grip. With a loose grip, begin to slowly move our hand up and down, with a movement of only about two inches. Gradually wave your hand faster, up and down, until an up-down cycle is about five times per second. The loose grip should allow the pencil to wobble between the thumb and forefinger. At about three to four cycles per second, notice the appearance of the pencil. You've succeeded when the pencil looks like it is bending.

The tail of the *Rhamphorhynchoid* was probably never meant to twitch like that of a cat that is watching a bird. I believe that the flexibility at the base of the *Rhamphorhynchoid* tail allows the creature to change flight direction quickly.

But the point is this: That place of flexibility corresponds precisely to the place of flexibility in the pencil-bending magic. Where the pterosaur tail connects to the pterosaur body—that corresponds to where the pencil end is held by thumb and forefinger, and when the tail is moved one way, the body will turn as well; compare it with the rudder and elevators of an air-plane tail. Even if the primary length of the *Rhamphorhynchoid* tail were 100% inflexible (it is not), its sudden movement would cause similarly relevant body-movement. Hand movement causes the pencil turning; but with the *Rhamphorhynchoid*, the tail movement causes the body turning. I believe that the optical illusion is the same. Why else would many of the eyewitnesses describe a straight tail for a creature flying in a straight direction but ZJ describes a flexible tail on a sparrow-catching creature?

I received an email from a lady [OJ] who had recently witnessed the flight of a "pterodactyl," at night in Ohio. She felt it especially eerie to have seen it on June 26, 2010, the night of a partial lunar eclipse.

At 11:15 p.m., she was driving near Kenton, Ohio, on Route 309. With clear sky and a still-full moon, the landscape was brightly lit. A creature swooped down—an obvious "pterodactyl"—gliding gracefully over the hood of her car. She watched it fly into some dense underbrush of trees.

Because of the brightness of the moon (several hours before the eclipse) and the nearness of the creature's flight, she saw it clearly. OJ was im-pressed with that slow smooth flight, with no wing flapping. She told me, "It was very eerie . . . Sent shivers over me." Her mind raced, trying to find some bird explanation, but to no avail. She wondered how she could report it, and asked me, "Is there a society to contact to report this to?"

Later that night of the sighting, OJ's daughter noticed the shock on her mother's face, and on hearing why, mentioned "a show on history chan-nel or discovery channel" in which eyewitnesses had seen similar flying creatures. OJ was embarrassed to mention the word "pterodactyl," but her daughter assured her that the same word was used on the television program. In her email to me, OJ said, "Then I knew I wasn't crazy for saying it." She also told me that the creature she had witnessed was huge but not as large as the ones in the *Jurassic Park* movie.

I found it interesting that she asked if a "society" existed for receiving her report, and that the word "pterodactyl" gave her, at first, embarrassment. In Western society, including the United States, dogmas of extinction cause eyewitnesses of live modern pterosaurs problems: "Who do I tell?" is common; recognizing and verbalizing "embarrassment" is uncommon. I am grateful for the broadcasts of *Destination Truth* and *Monsterquest,* for they revealed the possibility of flying creatures like "pterodactyls" (even though pertaining to New Guinea). I hope many American eyewitnesses will thereby come to trust their senses, even without embarrassment.

My reply: "Thank you, [OJ]. I am grateful you told me about your sighting. I have been writing about sightings of apparent pterosaurs since 2003, and have published two non-fiction books on the subject, so you were right to contact me. I would like to ask you a few questions, if that is OK."

Q) What was the weather like?

A) The weather was absolutely beautiful and calm with a bright full moon, not a cloud in the sky . . .

Q) How high above the ground was the creature flying?

A) It was about 10 feet up above my front hood of my car . . .

Q) Did it have a tail?

A) It looked like it had a tail [OJ later said that the tail was not long but "there was a tail"] and was also looking like it was jet black. I could see almost the bones in its wings but I did NOT see feathers at all. None. . . . it was bright out . . . because of the full moon being high in the sky.

Like many, but not all, eyewitnesses, OJ gave me many details, including her feelings about the encounter.

"I had my window [to the car] open because it was quite warm out. It startled me due to it coming so close to the front of my car . . . it swooped down at my hood but was still gliding and for the entire time I did not see it use its wings but only had a smooth glide. Very eerie.

"I was a little shook up when I saw it but only after the fact because I was still in a little shock and . . . couldn't wait to tell my daughter who was still only about 10 minutes away. I was traveling about 50 mph but it was perfect timing for it because it came from the left side of the highway out of some trees or near some trees and then by the time my car reached that exact spot where it was over my hood 10 feet up I would guess, it then kept on gliding to the right of the road . . . and towards a thick set of trees still off a little in the distance.

"I just can't get this out of my mind. I did not know who to contact about it either so thank you for your quick response. I'd be happy to show someone the exact spot it happened at, too. I mean strange things came to my mind like is *Jurassic Park* more real [than] just a movie because I know cloning goes on with various animal types but you know those crazy things enter ones mind when they see something like this. Take care, [OJ]"

Notice how this sighting resembles that of Susan Wooten's in South Carolina. I find nothing strange about the similarity of apparent pterosaurs flying right in front of cars of eyewitnesses. Remember we are examining mainly human reports, not pterosaur behaviors. When a pterosaur flies far above or behind a car, for that driver no flying creature is observed. When it flies right in front of the car—that is when it is seen to be a giant featherless creature that cannot be explained away as a bird or bat. That is when the person is more likely to get in touch with me and report the encounter; a distant maybe-pterosaur rarely motivates somebody to report it to a cryptozoologist like me. But a few close encounters suggest many distant appearances (rarely reported), and that suggests those creatures are not very rare: maybe nocturnal and only somewhat uncommon.

Another Ohio sighting, in 2005, was reported by a minister [OM], although I have not yet interviewed the man. In Mount Vernon, he was driving to a preaching assignment when he noticed something in the sky. He slowed to get a better look. He described it as a "leathery grayish color," with no sign of feathers. The beak was the same color as the rest of the head. The wings were not bird-like but bat-like. The strangest part was the tail: long, featherless, and with a "diamond-shaped point at the end."

The minister [OM] knew the birds of Ohio, including those of the Mount Vernon area. He noted that the featherless appearance, head, and tail of the creature differed greatly from the birds. In addition, he was sure it was larger than any Bald Eagle. Most ministers have no active involvement in creationism (in 2005, very few American ministers would have been aware of living-pterosaur investigations). They are not biased towards a pterosaur interpretation. Why doubt that this minister was making an objective evaluation? I believe that this sighting report is perfectly valid.

The year of this minister's sighting in Ohio, I received an email from a woman [NK] who saw a giant "pterodactyl" flying 300 miles to the east, over Philadelphia. I failed to get a detailed interview with her, but this account is credible enough to include for comparison with other accounts.

"Greetings. I am not sure if this will be of any help or even believable to you, but I [along with a friend] saw what we termed a pterodactyl.

"It was several years ago . . . approximately 5:00 A.M. . . . almost sure it was summer . . . The weird part is I live in Philly. [My friend] was dropping me off, and parked. . . . . . about six blocks away . . . we saw something that made our jaws drop. We were like 'what the h* is that thing?' This thing didn't seem to fly quickly. [Its] wingspan was huge. We'd figured at least 20 feet or so. It wasn't flapping real hard like a sparrow or pigeon does. It almost seemed to sail. It came from the South, and appeared to be heading west [towards the Delaware River].

"As God [is] my witness we saw this thing. . . . It had an anvil shaped head and somewhat of a long neck. . . . it didn't have a long tail sticking out from [its] back part.

"We told people what we saw and they said we were nuts. Also dismissed it as a hawk or eagle. We do have a hawk in my neighborhood. So I know what the heck that looks like. This thing had to be at least twice the size of a hawk. Maybe three times. I've seen . . . vultures down by the Delaware River, and this thing in no way looked like that or a crane. No way. If nobody else in Philly saw that thing then it's amazing because you could not miss it.

"If you ever get a chance can you let me know if any kind of pterosaur has been seen in a city? I will go to my death remembering that, and so will my friend . . . It freaked us out so bad." [end of account by NK]

Late in the summer of 2008, I received an email from a lady who lives in Winder, Georgia. She seems to have had the rare privilege of observing two pterosaurs, apparently different individuals of the same species, on two different days. The first flew right in front of the car she was driving.

In her email, she said, "Good evening, Mr Whitcomb. I have not yet read your book, *Searching for Ropens*; rather I came to your site by way of Google . . . and by way of many searches over the last few weeks."

The lady (I'll call her "PS") had been trying to find someone who might help her verify the existence of the strange animals that she had seen twice in the past few weeks. I believe, from what she told me, that she had two reasons: to confirm the anatomy of what she had seen, and to find someone else who had seen it.

Her first sighting was at 7 a.m., the second, 9 a.m., with both mornings overcast (she felt that significant, for with the sun in her eyes she might not have seen the creatures). Both times she phoned a friend to tell him of her extraordinary experience.

I replied, "Thank you, [PS] Yes, I would like to know about what you saw. Where did you see them? How many were there? Jonathan"

"Hi, Jonathan. Thank you so much for writing back to me, I wasn't sure you would. I do appreciate it.

"I live in a small town in northeast Georgia, called Winder . . . (I was a little hesitant to . . . mention being from Georgia because I don't want any-one to think uh-oh, has she got Bigfoot in the freezer too?)"

She told me a bit about Winder and about her commute, which is about twenty-five miles through a partially forested area.

Fifteen miles of her commute is on a two-lane 55-mph road through woods alternating with pastures; This part of Highway 82 has few houses and

The Winder, Georgia, sighting was only about 170 miles (straight line) from Susan Wooten's South Carolina sighting

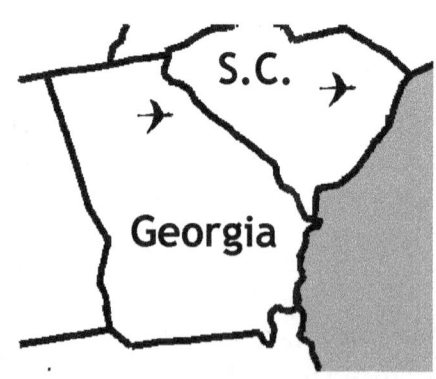

almost no stop signs. I presume her description of the country is typical of northwest Georgia: dense pine forests with some hardwood trees.

The southeastern United States had just been hit by Fay (a serious tropical storm that caused at least one drowning death in Georgia) when PS drove to work on August 27, 2008. She had woken up early and could not get back to sleep, so she left her house at 6:45 a.m., with the sky still overcast from the last remnants of the storm. I believe this weather disturbance may relate to her daylight encounter with an animal I believe to be nocturnal.

Commuting to work, she usually drives into the morning sun, with the car visor down, but it was unnecessary on August 27. She had driven less than ten miles, just leaving an area of pasture, entering an area of thick woods, around a mild downhill curve, with high banks and brush on each side of the road, when an animal suddenly flew from the right, just over the front of her car. Although alone, she yelled, "What the --- what --- what is that?" She was stunned.

She told me what made her yell out loud: It was the tail; she looked up at a "very long" tail that had a strange shape at the end. She later sent me some sketches (she is a professional artist but has not given me permission to publish the sketches), one of them showing a thick almost-heart-shape at the end of the tail; it differs from the usual "diamond" shape suggested by some eyewitnesses, but I believe this creature is related to the others.

Overall, the animal was tan, similar to the light brown of the local deer, and the color was uniform. The wings appeared half spread, and she was looking at its side, so she could not make an estimate of the wingspan.

"Dive-bombing my car," is how she described the flight path, as it crossed the highway in front of and slightly above her. "Curved, like a hammer," is how she described the head, which had a crest that she thought was "solid, not feathery at all." Her sketch showed a smoothly curved head crest.

A ridge runs along the underside of the tail; as I interpret her sketch, that prominent ridge extends about halfway into the "heart-shaped pad," but I allow some doubt in the certainty of her memory of that tail detail. The creature had "a fat tummy," but not fat enough to avoid being mostly obscured by wings. PS said, "The thing made perfect sense as it flew;" other eyewitness have also been struck by the gracefulness of flight.

She told me, "I was floored. I knew what it was. I couldn't believe what it was. But I knew what it was." Then began another type of encounter.

She phoned a friend whom she thought might be awake that early and started a conversation that was probably typical of many others between a pterosaur eyewitness and a trusted or trusting friend: It started with something like, "You won't believe what I just saw."

The lady told him about the "pterodactyl," to which he replied that she had probably seen a Great Blue Heron; maybe it was carrying a snake. The conflict she now encountered, not in the phone conversation but in her own reasoning (her inner voice), involved something like "Of course; something like that," versus "You know what you saw."

PS looked at the online page her friend had recommended and searched through online photos of herons and other birds . . . Negative. Everything about the bird photos was wrong, including the color and shape. Her friend later asked about planes; she pointed out that the creature flew under the tree tops. He asked, "Why hasn't anyone in Winder seen them?" She pointed out that she had just seen one. Eventually her friend proved his friendship: He stopped raising objections and admitted he could not explain what she had seen. I count this lady on the fortunate list, for not all friends, relatives, and family members are so kind.

Two weeks later, on September 10, PS overslept, getting out the door at 8:50 a.m., which bothered her. Each day, she hoped to get another view of the flying creature, assuming it only flew in that area at early morning. I agree with her concerning animal habits that can put them in certain areas at certain times; but I suspect this is an exception related to the recent storm. At any rate, PS had no hope of seeing the creature that morning, for she was driving much later than before. The lost opportunity bothered her.

The sky was again overcast as she left Winder. Just two miles out of town, however, as she came to a curve at the top of a gently flowing hill, at a little over a hundred yards away, she saw it: the same kind of creature but not the same individual; this one was bigger.

The treetop level below the hill, level with her car on the hill top—that is where the creature was "just flapping along:" right in front of her windshield, but further away from her than the first one was. This one flew only somewhat perpendicular to her drive; it was somewhat flying away. Again she could see a head crest; again, a long tail with a thick ending. This time PS took note that the tail did not hang down limp as if the creature were carrying a snake; it pointed back behind, making it an obvious part of the creature's body. That confirmed it: a long tail.

The wings "pumped" in a "scooping" manner, as the motion rippled along the body and through the tail. It was the same way with the first creature, reminding PS of some kind of "breast stroke." She was enthralled by the logic of that wing flapping, different from that of birds: Wings of birds appear to flap more up-and-down. She told me that the creatures she had seen appeared to grab the air and pull themselves through it.

As PS was writing her email to me, she realized the significance of that rippling motion in the creature's body. The animal must have been huge, "bigger than a big dog and probably longer than a man is tall." She decided that the one she had seen on August 27 was as long as her Camry is wide, and second one, the length of her Camry.

On September 10, she slowed her car while gazing at the creature as it flew away. Expecting nothing on that morning, she became one of the few, of which I am aware, who have seen a living pterosaur on two occasions. She tried to express to me her feelings about the second one: "I was blown away." She again phoned her friend, who asked if it might have been a Pileated Woodpecker. She replied, "No . . . not a woodpecker." (I think this animal should be called "American Hammerhead Ropen.")

I believe it was the second sighting which prompted her to communicate with me. It must have convinced her of the reality of the first encounter and that the animal was what it appeared to be. I am grateful, not just for details of information: for her personal reconciliation with the truth of her encounter with a living being that our cultural traditions keep hidden.

The lady used to dread her daily commute to work; that has changed. She told me, "The world is now totally different. I feel blessed that God has allowed me to see this creature that should not be here, and yet is, this strange dragon-like thing that lives somewhere in the woods in this red-neck little town." I feel that God will bless all Americans through people like this lady, who share these wonderful experiences with us.

She soon became excited about new questions: Are these animals local or were they blown in by the storm? Where and when do they sleep? What do they eat? I suspect she had originally been excited about the first question, the one faced by many American eyewitnesses of living pterosaurs: "Does that experience make one crazy?" I will continue to encourage eyewitnesses to stop questioning their sanity; question incorrect traditions. But the questions about living pterosaurs themselves I find hard to answer.

PS believes that the animals' coloring prevents anyone from seeing them when they are at rest in a forest and that large active animals need "serious food" to fly like that. Another friend suggested a diet of rodents (they're plentiful in town) and told PS that she had recently heard something strange in the woods near her house, something like a hawk in extreme distress. She had also once seen the shadow of something like a very large bird flying into the woods in the evening. Those observations may be helpful.

PS had some doubts about nocturnal living, for the animals she has seen (in daylight) have small eyes. Taking another perspective, if many of these animals flew regularly in daylight I would be swamped with daily emails from eyewitnesses; this is not the case, so I suspect they are nocturnal.

I informed my associate, SMW, of the sightings by PS. He replied:

"That's interesting about the East Coast sightings. I've done quite a lot of research over the years on supposed sightings out here, but had no results. I was actually [traveling] last weekend to a . . . site . . . I've been to many times, and spent all night hiking and observing, but . . . saw nothing. I don't think there's enough evidence to build much of a case for them living around here. I enjoyed e-mailing Susan Wooten a while back (thank you for the contact, by the way) and don't doubt her trustworthiness, but wonder if the pterosaur she sighted was just migrating through from somewhere else (I imagine they could fly all the way from PNG or Africa, since some birds go these distances)."

I replied to SMW, "Thank you for your continued investigations. It seems there are few of us actively looking for living pterosaurs, regardless of how many cryptozoologists are actively looking for various cryptids. The significance of the two Georgia sightings are that they were only a few days ago and a few days apart and of two different creatures of the same description (but different size) and in the same area and flying in daylight. I understand, however, your challenge at the moment [finances]."

Before leaving Georgia, another lady (I've not interviewed her), reported a "thunderbird" with a wingspan of about ten feet and a "single white line around its neck." This reminded me of other sightings of what seem to be true birds, large or giant, with feathers. (Thunderbirds are investigated by Gerhard.) But I include this report here because DD said it was: "not . . . feathery, more like leathery." Whatever it was, it scared her.

In mid-2007, a man in New Mexico emailed me about his two sightings.

"Hello, my name is [RA] and I live in central N.M.. Fourteen years ago, in [Socorro], N.M., me and a close friend, who now has a masters in biology, were hiking during the midday sun at [a] box canyon and something blocked the sun for a moment. We both looked up to see what did that and saw a large flying animal.

"It had a 20-30 foot wingspan and was about the same length long. It had a long tail with [a] seeming spike at the end. Its head was very pterodactyl shape with a fluted back pointy head. It glided at about 700 feet in a westward direction. It was black and we watched it glide . . . and land somewhere on the southern expanse of Magdalena Mountains.

"I never thought that there would be a place to really tell someone about it. Last night on TV, there was a discussion about the strange sightings of a flying animal on the local news. If you have any idea of what we might have seen, tell me. I saw it again in the same sort of conditions a month later after the first sightings."

I replied, "Thank you for telling me about your sightings, [RA]"

Q: What part of the year was it?

A: When I saw it, it was . . . midday, no clouds (March or April).

Q: When you saw the creature one month later, was the time of day and weather the same?

A: Both times it seemed to land in the same place and both times the conditions and time were the same.

Q: How long was the tail? (half the wingspan? More? Less?)

A: As I recall the tail was much longer than the wingspan. We joked for years that we saw a dragon.

Q: Can you tell me more about the local news report of a flying animal?

A: It was the local news 13, a CBS channel. If you look on the internet it will be KRQE. The story went something like this . . . A man alone in the Dona Ana Mountains, a mtn. range just north of the Las Cruces, was walking during the day in the desert along the base of the mountain . . . he saw two of the pterodactyl like creatures. They were sitting on the ridge top watching him, then flew towards and over him. He described them much the same as I did. He said [it was] about ten years ago. I am not sure what inspired the local newscast to do the show last Thursday. [end of answer to the question about the news report]

RA added, "There are also a myriad of other little stories I have heard but have not mentioned since they are a bit vague. I used to tell people that I had seen a dragon twice in the wild but never a mountain lion. In Soccoro there is a local legend that an animal similar in description to what we are speaking [about] frequents the gravel pits near the Rio Grande River. We conjectured that it might have a gizzard. (?)"

Early in 2008, I received an email from man who reported a pair of *ropen*-like creatures in the state of Washington. His account of the 1987 sightings included some descriptions that differed from those by other eyewitnesses, and our communications were cut short, so I was not able to verify his credibility to the degree that I would have liked; still, the plausibility that he had honestly reported two living pterosaurs that he did encounter—that appears significant enough to justify inclusion here. More likely than not, he told the truth, and that is what he encountered. GW is anonymous.

"I was 15 yrs old [when] I saw two ropens together sitting on a fence. I was riding my bike home from a friend's house around 5 pm in [a town in southwest Washington state]. I lived in the country with my parents on a . . . ranch. I was approx. $1/2$ mile from home, riding down an old country road . . . just south of [town]. I heard a strange noise [a kind of] screech.

"I looked to my left, and on a wood plank fence were two of the biggest bird-like creatures I could ever imagine! I almost crashed my bike! They were about 50 ft from me; the first thing I noticed was their heads, then I thought this can't be! Could they be dinosaurs? . . .

"When I was a kid, all I knew is what I saw in the history books, movies, etc... plus I was an eagle lover: I used to draw eagles a lot, an so I knew what I saw. I stood on the road and watched them for about an hour. One was hopping off the fence and appeared like it was teasing the other one.

"They were huge! [Their feet] wrapped around a 2"x6" plank; I just couldn't believe it! [Their] heads I would have to say it was maybe 4 ft long with the beak. . . . a brown body color that looked like hair . . . the wings looked like black rubber. Their tails were curled up but were maybe 6 ft long . . . I was so scared they might hear me or fly towards me.

"If [you're] interested I will tell you what I did, and how they reacted. To make a long story short, I found where they stayed near the house I grew up in. I told my mom and she saw them too, and took their pictures. That was 21 yrs ago... Hope that helps with your search for the ropen. If you want to hear more, let me know . . ."

I soon replied to GW's email:

"Thank you for letting me know about your sightings. Yes, I would like to know more about it. Was it about 1987? About how long were their wing-spans? (wingtip-to-wingtip) Thank you."

GW replied the same day:

"Hi Johnathon. Yes it was 1987; I was a sophomore in high school. I want you to know if I would have had someone other [than] my mother to talk to about them we would have mentioned it. But my mother was worried no one would believe it.

"I can tell you I believe their wing span was about 20 ft tip to tip. These creatures didn't fly very high up when we first saw them, they don't glide much either. We were able to follow where they landed after leaving the fence; it was behind our ranch to a pond where a neighbor grew trout. We watched them there for a little while until they flew into some . . . heavily brushed area about 1 mile behind our house.

"I used to trap back in that area when I was young, so I grabbed my 22 rifle an walked down the trails. I still heard a screeching type noise, enough to make your skin crawl.

"I can tell you these ropens heads looked a little different then what others described. The thing on the back of their heads looked like HMMM more spooned shape and narrow on the head side and wider on the other end. They did notice me at one point, and these creatures were nesting on the ground! Not in the trees, but in a brushy woodsy area near a small aban-doned home.

"It's strange my mom and I used to say, I wonder if those monsters ate the people that lived there! . . . they just up and left; we knocked at the door but it was clear no one was living there . . . [their] stuff was still in place.

"I recently moved . . . to Longview, WA, which is only . . . minutes from the sightings. I think I will go to the area again and see if I find anything. Who knows, maybe I will find a nest, or a whole colony..UGH.. I think I'll take the shot gun this time.

"It's nice to see that there has been other sightings, and I'm not crazy! I told my girlfriend about them 10 yrs ago but I had never seen any info of other sightings until recently. If you want to talk on the phone, you are welcome to call me at my house I am usually home anytime after 6 PM. If you are ever in the area, I can also take you out there. Sincerely [GW]"

I said nothing to GW about night sightings of flying lights in Washington and he said nothing about night sightings to me, so I have no way yet to connect his sighting report with bioluminescent flying creatures.

We exchanged a few more emails, but GW stopped replying to my questions soon after I mentioned paying for duplicating his photos (assuming he would be able to find the old photos). His friend, who had also seen the creatures (at about the time he had), advised him that he should not have told anyone else. One of the last things GW said to me was "I don't want people banging down my door for answers."

I realize that critics may suggest that this man stopped answering my questions because he had no photographs to show me. Nevertheless, I noticed a number of things that indicated to me that he was telling the truth. We need to remember the innumerable hiding places available for a less-common flying creature in the vast forests of the state of Washington; in light of the many other sighting reports of apparent pterosaurs, long-tailed and "huge," we also need to understand that a present lack of photographs is hardly evidence for any hoax or combination of hoaxes: GW appears to have told me the truth.

The "curled up" tails struck me, but only with a glancing blow. If GW saw only a slight curl of the tail, the two creatures could have been *Rhamphorhynchoid* pterosaurs. I wish that GW had stayed with me; I wouldn't mind being struck by glancing at the photographs (assuming he'd found them).

In the Spring of 2009, after I had analyzed similarities between the many reports of sightings in the United States, it became obvious that no hoax (or combination of hoaxes) was involved. Pterosaurs live in the United States, not as migrants or stragglers: They live here as residents. It also became obvious that at least some of the strange flying lights, in various states, might be from creatures similar to the *ropen* of Papua New Guinea.

Chapter 4

Flying Luminescence

Three weeks after I had finished exploring south-central Umboi Island, Papua New Guinea (2004), two other Americans camped a few kilometers to the north. At 10 o'clock one night, while Garth Guessman was meeting with leaders of nearby Arot Village, David Woetzel was watching the sky. A strange glowing object flew from the direction of one mountain, disappearing behind another. Unlike a meteor, the large globe, twinkling around the edges, moved closer to horizontally. Any meteor that large should have left a trail behind it, but this flying light left no trail: literally un-meteoric.

One year later, Woetzel wrote a scientific paper for the Creation Research Society Quarterly (Volume 42, March 2006): ". . . a spine-tingling sight—a glowing object passing low on the horizon from the direction of Mt. Barik and disappearing behind Mt. Tolou [Tolo] . . . moved quickly—almost like a shooting star. But it was unlike any [meteor] I had ever seen . . . a large, yellowish glow approximately 20-25% the size of the full moon."

It lasted only a few seconds, too brief to power up the camcorder. But Woetzel's experience with the *ropen* light vindicated the many native eyewitnesses whose limited English had made it difficult to describe. But the many interviews we conducted in those two expeditions revealed that the *ropen* light of Umboi flies close to horizontally, just above the tree canopy, often from one mountain to another or from Mount Bel to-or-from the coast. A few eyewitnesses have been close enough to distinguish features, including a long tail; but those "lucky" sightings are few.

Flying lights attributed to large flying creatures—they also appear in other parts of Papua New Guinea. On the mainland, in a village near the city of Wau, its called "seklo-bali;" further inland (west) near Tawa Village, it's called "indava." On the coast (east of Wau), at Salamaua, similar lights fly at night. The Baptist missionary Jim Blume saw a small glowing form one night: on a ridge above a mangrove swamp on the coast of Manus Island, north of Umboi Island. Luminous flying creatures seem to be widespread in Papua New Guinea. We now call them "ropens." But is there another explanation? Could they be something other than living pterosaurs?

Fred Silcock, of Victoria, Australia, has made a unique study of the barn owl, *Tyto alba*. For years, he studied eyewitness accounts of what some Australians call the *Min Min*. He concluded that the strange wandering lights observed occasionally in certain parts of Australia are a rare intrinsic bioluminescent glow of some barn owls.

Why do there seem to be no reports of pet owls or zoo owls that glow? Part of the answer may be in the wild, for some of the owls that glow have been found to be distressed, in particular hungry. Some eyewitness accounts of the *Min Min* lights include descriptions that suggest that a barn owl is catching insects. Well-fed birds in cages have no need to glow.

The research by Silcock discounts the notion that the glow of some barn owls comes from a luminous fungus in some tree hollows where the birds roost. Most luminous fungi require moisture, so a dusty residue on the wings of a bird in flight would not likely glow at all, especially not as brightly as described; in addition, birds normally keep their feathers clean. And in the arid parts of Australia where *Min Mins* are more often seen, the luminous fungi are absent.

But an intrinsic glow means an owl has conscious or unconscious control, and native bioluminescence in a bird means energy would be required to produce the light. I believe that the distant ancestors of modern barn owls used bioluminescence as a common aid in their hunting, and many generations of successful hunting with little need for it have reduced it to a rare tool, triggered, perhaps, when some owls are especially hungry. The world-wide range of *Tyto alba* shows how successful this owl has been.

I have carefully read Mr. Silcock's book *The Min Min Light: The Visitor Who Never Arrives*. The substantial eyewitness evidence and his reasoning have convinced me of his conclusions: A few barn owls sometimes glow.

How does this relate to glowing *ropens*? The common barn owl, long officially classified by Western science, has been shown, by much eye-witness evidence, to have intrinsic bioluminescence, although it is rarely used by owls and rarely declared in textbooks. The Komodo Dragon, long officially declared non-venomous, was found to be venomous while I was writing the first edition of this book. Science progresses. "Glowing pterosaurs" has been emphasized by one critic to dismiss our investigations, for it makes our case appear too weird. But if a common classified bird can glow, why not a rare unclassified cryptid? And if the long-declared-non-venomous Komodo Dragon is discovered to be venomous, what next?

Nevertheless, with glowing barn owls misidentification is a concern, for the *Min Min* light flies in Australia, just south of where the *ropen* light flies in Papua New Guinea. Could "glowing pterosaurs" be a mistake? Know the details, understand the relationships. This deserves a close look.

In Australia, when someone gets a close look at a *Min Min*, they see a *Great Owl*; in Papua New Guinea, when someone gets a close look at a *ropen* light, they see a long-tailed pterosaur. That is the main point. But additional points confirm the *ropen*-owl difference.

How does the *Min Min* differ? It never descends to the surface of the sea regularly (like it's fishing on a reef), but far inland. It never glows brightly enough to light up Tarawe Village on Umboi Island, but only enough to catch insects at the feet of a horse on a dirt road in the Australian outback.

The old stories about *ropen* grave-robberies appear to be nonfiction. Why? We interviewed native eyewitnesses who mentioned particular funerals of particular deceased humans: Michael, of Opai Village, told me about a man who was buried at Gomlongon Village in 1949; Eunice, the school-teacher's wife, told Carl Baugh about the funeral on the northwest coast of Umboi Island in April, 1993. In both cases, the glowing *ropen* flew down towards the burial location, although in 1993 the mourners scared away the *ropen*; in 1949, the *ropen* carried away the body to a mountain, so that it could be alone to . . . well, you get the point: We accuse no barn owl.

Daylight reveals the fallacy of "misidentification" on a dark night, a favored conjecture of critics. In Papua New Guinea, both the American Duane Hodgkinson and the Australian Brian Hennessy saw, in daylight, creatures nobody would mistake for an owl: long tail, head crest, feather-less appearance. And on Umboi Island, by the shore of Lake Pung, seven native boys saw "ropen;" there was no mistaking, in daylight, the long tail and "no feathers." There is no way an American would see a barn owl with a tail "at least" 10-15 feet long and a native would see another barn owl with a tail "sefan meetah" (about twenty-two feet) long. There were no mistakes on dark nights, in those cases, for there was no night, no dark.

How do we know that giant *Rhamphorhynchoid*-like creatures seen, but rarely, in daylight are those glowing at night? On Umboi Island, we rely not just on the native traditions. Jonathan Ragu and Jonah Jim, at different times and different places on Umboi, saw a large creature that they later associated with a sketch of a *Sordes Pilosus* pterosaur. Both men described a flying creature that was glowing, as did the school-teacher's wife.

But that subject is explored in my book *Searching for Ropens*. How do bioluminescence *ropens* in Papua New Guinea relate to pterosaurs in the United States? How could giants of a tropical wilderness live among us? Consider another perspective. How could a species of giant flying creature be prevented, for thousands of years, from gradually establishing breeding locations in North America? That question deserves attention.

Some birds migrate for many thousands of miles. I have personally experienced, without personal wings, a long flight over the Pacific Ocean. Since humans were inspired by birds to invent flying machines, give credit to birds for that inspiration. And give credit to the lowly Monarch Butterfly for migrating in large numbers for 2000 miles, with individuals crossing the Atlantic Ocean sometimes. But the wings of a giant *ropen* make the whole planet accessible, with little to fear . . . except human bullets.

Perhaps the longest part of the journey from Kitty Hawk to the moon was between 1903 and 1908, when the Wright brothers were labeled "liars." Few humans indeed were flying during those five years. But mud slinging becomes less hazardous to the flyers who gain altitude; those who stoop to grab more mud remain ignorant of what flies overhead even if they could avoid the mud that falls back into their own eyes. Unfortunately for mudslingers, they themselves usually sleep in daylight and sling in the dark.

But what makes bioluminescence important to the concept of pterosaurs living in the United States? Bioluminescence helps *ropens* fly at night, and a rare nocturnal *ropen* in the United States should very rarely appear in daylight, revealing a pterosaur-form. It is that extreme rarity of appearance that would cause a few eyewitnesses to appear crazy or dishonest, and the "liar" appearance could hide an American *ropen* from official discovery for centuries. This, I believe, has happened. Whether labeled "dragon," "ropen," or "pterosaur," it has only recently been acknowledged a cryptid, and it may be a long journey to graduate from cryptozoology to biology.

We now have evidence for rare nocturnal bioluminescent flying creatures in the United States; nevertheless, because form or features are rarely seen, and locations may be widely separated (with local residents being mostly ignorant of similar lights outside their locality), the flying lights have been given various labels and explanations.

Chapter 5

American Ghost Lights

While doing an online search, in 2007, I came across a letter by one of the living-pterosaur investigators (later I realized that it was not intended for the general public). Never before had so many apparent *ropen* lights been observed by investigators, even more than in Paul Nation's 2006-2007 expeditions. I asked the investigator about the sightings; we'd previously always shared information freely, but he now told me only the results of their investigation, not the location. Perhaps unaware that the online letter could be easily found, he had posted information that he and his associates thought would remain secret. Still, the location of the extraordinary *ropen*-light displays, especially secret, was left out of the online letter.

Secrecy in scientific research and development, an accepted practice, has been common for generations. This was no exception. The location of the mid-2007 expedition I promised to keep secret; the investigator gave me more than one reason to justify secrecy, and, since I found nothing inappropriate in this case, I kept location-details out of my writings. Nevertheless, without revealing location or names of main investigators, I feel that the fruit of their work needs to be revealed.

In the summer of 2007, several cryptozoologists accepted the invitation to stay at the home of a man whose property is visited by at least two kinds of nocturnal flying creatures. For years, the man had observed what he had first assumed were shooting stars. He paid closer attention when he noticed that some of the flying lights moved up instead of down, and some even turned in flight. Eventually he learned about living-pterosaur investigations and communicated with my associates.

A few years earlier, the man (I'll call him FJ) had found, in daylight, a strange creature on his property. With a wingspan of about seven feet, it had claws on the wings and a crest on the head. At the end of its tail was something he described in terms we investigators associate with a *Rhamphorhynchoid* pterosaur. Only later did the man connect the creature with the flying lights.

Just days before the arrival of the cryptozoologists, FJ observed the flying lights over a body of water near his home: a brilliant display, at 10-11 p.m., that concentrated in one area. He heard piercing cries that he assumed came from the flying creatures.

The cryptozoologists were not disappointed, with many sightings of the flying lights and a few sightings of the forms of large flying creatures that were unlike bats. One of them flew close enough that one man almost fell over. The men stayed only a few nights, but the investigation continued into 2008, with a number of visits to this location.

A flying bioluminescent thing can escape notice, unseen or mistaken for a meteor, but I received an email from a person I call "DU." He did notice.

"I and two other people had an extremely interesting experience fishing at night along a river. I will not tell you the exact location . . . at least not yet, because it is a remote portion of the mid-U.S. and I want it to stay that way. It happened Aug 21, 2008 . . . midnight.

"We had turned off our lantern and were fishing when we all three saw a small creature that was flying very fast . . . but the catch was it was glowing off and on, off and on (otherwise we would have never seen it). It darted around much like a bat, but was faster than any bat I've ever seen. I've seen swallows dive as fast as it, but the object wasn't diving but rather moving horizontally across the tops of the river bank trees and out along the middle of the river. The glowing portion of the object was only [6-8 inches], but it must have had wings too. It came within 30 ft from us and was probably only 20 ft off the [water's] surface.

"The glowing wasn't like a flash light's on and off, but more of a weird flickering until the object was in an intense greenish (like a [lightning] bug) glowing color. The on-off cycle lasted around 3-4 seconds and would start up again after the same amount of time not glowing. We could not make out a definite shape of the thing, because it was pitch black outside. It did seem to be gliding, because birds and bats alike have at least a little up and down to [their] flights due to wing beats; this object's flight path was smooth like a glider.

"Well, it disappeared down the river and we continued fishing. The object returned, exhibiting the same characteristics as mentioned, [about] twice more during the course of an hour. Each time it visited our area, it hung around for around 30-40 seconds.

". . . Over and over we asked ourselves what on this planet could possibly fit the description of what [we] were seeing. It did not seem to care we were there, and went along with its aerial hunting; I'm not sure what it was after." [end of DU's account]

According to F. F. Silcock (author of a book about the *Min Min* light of Australia) flying lights can be closer than they seem. If that were true with the sighting by DU, it would explain how the creature flew so fast while gliding: It was not really flying so fast. Regardless, a fast glide (or apparent fast glide) differs from the wandering flutter of a hunting owl, and the on-off cycle differs from the steady glow of a *Min Min* owl. It is strange.

In addition, we need to consider the possibility that the smoothness of the glowing creature's flight was not from gliding but from a smoother type of wing beating. Following the *ropen* hypothesis, a *Rhamphorhynchoid*'s wing beats may differ from those of both birds and bats.

Late in 2007, I received an email from Peter Beach, a biology professor. He had gone on two expeditions into Africa (searching for the *Mokele-mbembe* cryptid), before becoming involved in living-pterosaur research.

"I went on a short trip to the Yakima River this summer . . . because there was a [sighting]. We were unable to get a picture but we saw many . . . flashing lights. I would have assumed that [they] were fireflies but we [don't] have them in Washington. One of the flashes took off from a big tree overhanging the river and made a kind of flashing coma turn. Many flashes were parallel to the river. The river at that point [has] a crook . . . and there were many fish . . . Prime hunting grounds for fish-eating birds. Only these things fish at night with bioluminescence. At first I thought I was just seeing shooting stars, but they were all parallel to the river and close to the horizon. Next I noticed that when the cloud cover came in, I could still see the flashes. They were under the cloud cover. Whatever they are, I suggest that they are at least unknown to science, night flying, bioluminescent, flying creatures about the size of an eagle or big hawk, with a head knot . . . [appears] to be a "weird bird" as it perched in the tree, according to our confidant in Washington [State] who drives by the tree to work. Says he saw it a couple of times this summer, early in the morning. Blessing to you, Pete." [end of his account of the 2007 expedition]

I replied, "Thank you for mentioning the investigations [living-pterosaur concept in general] to your students . . . That is fascinating about the lights around the Yakima River. I have had a number of U.S. sighting reports since I last communicated with you. Wonderful!"

In August of 2008, I received another email from the professor: "During the short expedition I led with the O'Donnells, mid-July, we saw three hours of bioluminescent 'shooting stars.' The last hour was the most interesting in that there were two light blasts about 200 ft. apart, about 50-100 ft., above the river. The blasts were followed by screeches from about a dozen or so agitated nighthawks in the general area. I think the Rhamphorhynchoids, if that is what they were, were feeding on the nighthawks as the nighthawks were feeding on the flying insects. Bats were also common, but they were fast, made sharp turns, and were relatively small."

By this time Professor Beach knew about my conjecture that some *ropens* eat bats. I don't know if he looked for evidence of that on this expedition.

[Continuation of the email from Beach] "If bats were eaten, I have no evidence, since the audible sounds they make are relatively faint and higher pitched. I am familiar with the kinds of bats in Oregon and Washington and I can assure you there is no bat remotely like the size of what I saw." [referring to the creature he now describes]

"The shape of the flying animal I saw was 3-4 ft. wingspan, 2-3 ft. long, with a bat-like wing. The neck/head was obvious but only in silhouette, and I could not make out a tail or feet. If the tail is thin, I probably was not close enough to see it even if it was there. The wing beat rate caused me to arrive at the size and altitude. The wing [beat] was similar to a Canadian Goose; a seagull beats its wings faster, a Nighthawk (wingspan 18 in.) faster still."

Regarding the two flashes of light that were estimated to be 200 ft. apart, I asked the professor, "Were these two flashes . . . simultaneous? . . . Did they last about the same length of time? Was there anything unusual about the screeches from the Nighthawks?"

He replied, "As to the screeching of the Nighthawks. These birds make some noise almost all the time. Like they are talking to one another. [He later gets into more detail about the birds] The blast of light was like a 500 watt bulb flashed for about a half second . . . The second flash [was] of identical duration and intensity and occurred about two seconds apart. Since the flash was not blurred I would assume the animal or animals were briefly hovering. The screeching of the Nighthawks then took on a louder more urgent calling. The flashes set off all the birds at once, and the sky in the general vicinity was full of sound for about five seconds. The screeching then calmed down and there were no lights [or] unusual sounds for maybe five to ten minutes. It was about then the 'big bat' flew from about twenty feet above the river directly in front of me, and headed directly over my head. No lights but I got a great look at its silhouette against the Milky Way. . . ." [end of professor's account of his 2008 expedition]

I later read the account of a young man who was with Professor Beach in his second expedition. Phillip O'Donnell gave his version in an online cryptozoology forum: "We arrived (Peter, my brother Tim, & myself) . . . a couple of hours before sundown . . . About 12:40 a.m. I closed my eyes . . . Peter shook me wide awake. I looked up and saw a large black form shoot over me. Peter told me that he saw the creature for about 3 seconds as it came by. . . . He estimated that it flew 30 feet above our heads and that it had a wingspread of no less than 4 feet. The wings were almost the same as a bat. However, it had a long neck and beak. . . ." [no location given]

I'm sure that similar flying lights have been observed by Americans for generations, in many states. They've been given various names: *ghost lights, spook lights, earth lights,* the *Brown Mountain Light, Hornet Spooklight, Marfa Lights*. They've been given various explanations: ball lightning, UFO's, methane gas, tectonic stress (release of energy from underground). But the "dragon" explanation, mostly accounts from earlier centuries, would have been dismissed as unscientific in recent generations, dismissed as a ridiculous idea of common people, even if eyewitnesses had told scientists of a "dragon" seen near where the lights were seen.

Nineteenth-century American observers of strange lights could not have foreseen twentieth-century research on *Min Mins* or *ropens*, and few Americans in the twentieth century had heard of glowing barn owls or glowing pterosaurs. But we can now examine descriptions of *ghost lights* with more hope for more reasonable explanations. What? Did I say "more reasonable?" How can "glowing pterosaurs," formerly called "dragons," be more reasonable than scientific-sounding "methane" and "tectonic stress?" Consider the details in the descriptions, then decide for yourself if living bioluminescent flying organisms (birds, bats, or pterosaurs) make more sense than apparently scientific-sounding explanations.

Professor Beach, young Phillip O'Donnell, and a few other Americans have examined details in the testimonies of eyewitnesses of glowing pterosaur-like creatures in the southwest Pacific. We have concluded that the *ropen* is a pterosaur, and most (if not all) of the investigators believe that this creature has intrinsic bioluminescence. Of course this does not mean that every strange flying light in North America is of a *Rhamphorhynchoid* pterosaur. Careful consideration of the writings of Mr. Silcock will convince most readers that some flying lights, when they resemble the flights of hunting barn owls, may indeed be glowing owls. But when flying lights behave as if they were bioluminescent winged creatures, but not like hunting barn owls, we need to consider the obvious possibility: They may be winged creatures unacknowledged by science; one of those scientifically-unacknowledged winged creatures is the *ropen*.

I do not advocate cursory labeling of a *ghost light* "ropen." I advocate comparing American *ghost-light* descriptions with the overall accounts of *ropens* in the southwest Pacific. When a pterosaur-like creature is seen in the same area where *ghost lights* appear, consider whether those lights, in that area, differ in behavior from owl-behavior. If so, do the lights behave as if they were winged creatures? If so, consider the obvious: Those lights may have been from those pterosaur-like creatures. When all conditions apply, we dare suggest that those lights, there, are *ropens* or pterosaurs.

American *ghost lights* can be hard to explain, even for investigators who use the labels "Min Min" and "ropen." A problem rarely considered is eyewitness labeling. An eyewitness may see a light that seems strange, but the label of "strange" does not mean that the source of that light must be the same for all strange lights in that area.

Take the *Yakima Lights* of Washington State. When I first did an online search with "Yakima Lights," I assumed that the resulting report was of the same phenomenon as that observed by Peter Beach. But an investigation by Dr. Greg Little seems to have shown that some lights observed at the Yakima Reservation are what he calls "earthquake lights" or "earthlights." These were seen and photographed above fault lines, although they were said to have almost ceased after the Mt. Saint Helens volcanic eruption in 1980. I've done a cursory reading of some of his writings; his explanation for those lights that were investigated seem plausible to me.

But what are "Yakima Lights?" Apparent bioluminescent flying creatures, appearing to chase Nighthawks over the Yakima River, are not what Dr. Little has researched. How do they relate to *earth lights* over fault lines? They probably don't. Here we need to recognize that the word "Yakima," with its general reference to certain areas of Washington State, makes a coincidental relationship between two kinds of strange lights in the Northwest United States. We need not search for a deep relationship between car headlights, airplane lights, and trick-or-treat flashlights on October 31st; obviously they are commonplace. But we likewise need not search for a deep relationship between two different kinds of strange lights in Washington State, simply because they are labeled "strange" and they may include the word "Yakima." A humble admission that our scientists may yet make many discoveries in the future—that allows us to objectively evaluate two uncommon, different lights. And the distinctness of those differences gives us the answer: difference sources.

Dr. Michael Persinger has investigated *earth lights* and related phenomena for years. I've read none of his writings, so I make no comment on his conclusions except one aspect of one of his reported ideas: that *earth lights* may sometimes cause hallucinations. Whatever value that idea may or may not have, it is irrelevant to these living-pterosaur investigations. Those who have seen a clear form of an apparent living pterosaur had not been exposed to any strange light at the time, almost without exception; eyewitnesses of strange flying lights that investigators associate with pterosaurs or possible pterosaurs—those eyewitnesses saw no clear pterosaur-form, almost without exception. Any hallucination hypothesis vanishes.

Let's apply this to the Beach-O'Donnell sighting of 2008. The professor mentioned a 5-10 minute delay between the two brilliant flashes and the appearance of the flying creature that was too large for a local bat. This creature was also seen flying overhead by O'Donnell (and described by him as having a long neck and long beak). Obviously these two men were not the victims of a light that caused simultaneous and similar hallucinations with a precise time-delay; obviously we cannot question the Nighthawks to determine if they were screaming because of a large flying creature or only their hallucination of one. But the nature of those lights flying over the river, darting in various directions as if hunting bats or Nighthawks—that answers the non-biological *earth light* question: No.

Could they have seen hunting barn owls, glowing like *Min Mins* described by Silcock? The glaring problem with that explanation is in the combination of long neck and long beak: One might be dismissed as observational error, but not so reasonably both. Consider the details about the lights and the problems are magnified. Silcock described nothing like shooting stars. *Min Mins* appear as individuals or pairs, glowing mostly continuously as they flutter. They often stop to rest while still glowing, and when one flies overhead, it reveals itself: an owl. I don't say it's impossible for any owls to learn to hunt bats or Nighthawks; but it stretches the imagination to say they've stretched out their necks and beaks, and changed glow patterns.

What about the sighting by DU (also in mid-2008)? He saw no clear shape of what produced the light. Neither did he mention any eyewitness of a "strange bird" seen in that area in daylight, in contrast to the Yakima River area. But he saw a light flying unlike an owl and unlike an *earth light*; his description suggests a biologically-unclassified intrinsically-bioluminescent creature. . . . I hope he goes fishing again and sends me good news.

What about the night-light sightings by Susan Wooten? I was thrilled at first learning about her experiences with the *Bingham Lights*; my thrill faded when I realized that the swamp is fifty miles from where she had the daylight sighting, making it only a tenuous correlation. I've read other accounts of nighttime sightings in northeastern South Carolina, where curious young persons assume they've found the same swamp others have found. Some of the stories suggest a resemblance to *Min Mins*; others, not as much. What they may have in common is eyewitness-belief that they've all been to the same swamp and seen the *Bingham Lights*.

Nevertheless, a number of descriptions of flying lights, in that area of South Carolina, do suggest something other than owls. If I were living in the Southeast, I would be *ghost light* hunting, and regularly.

But regardless of the possibility of more than one swamp, regardless of the possibility of more than one source for all the lights, regardless of the possibility that the rumor is true about landowners cutting down trees in one of those swamps, I still have hope that those apparent nocturnal flyers will find swamps in which to survive, near Bingham or not: The Southeast has lots of swamps, even enough to hide rare nocturnal creatures not yet discovered, even if *Bingham Lights* are not pterosaurs.

Chapter 6

Marfa Lights of Texas

James was driving through Texas one night (about February 23, 2010), on his way to deliver a boat he was hauling to California. Like others driving through Marfa, the young man stopped at the viewing platform, hoping the dancing lights would appear. He had a special perspective, however, for he knew of my investigations, giving him an insight that allowed an unorthodox interpretation of some *ghost lights*: modern living pterosaurs.

The young man was prepared for disappointment, for *Marfa Lights* appear only a few times a year; but he was delighted, for the lights were active.

At 4:15 a.m. the sky was clear; the air, far below freezing. Near a tower that had a red blinking light, he saw two pulsating lights, much brighter than stars, similar in brightness to the tower light. At first the flashes were random, more on than off. James noticed a color shift towards red but they were "80% white." Afterwards he had no memory of their movement. They appeared for a few minutes then were gone for awhile.

From the Marfa Lights Viewing Platform (MLVP), he estimated that the two lights were somewhat west of directly south. Directions do make a difference here, for to the southwest or west-by-southwest, car headlights on Highway 67 fool many tourists: Atmospheric effects play tricks on headlights. There is a ranch road in the direction James said he saw those two lights, but he doubts that those two lights were headlights.

From about 4:30 a.m. until about 7:00 a.m., he observed another light, apparently further away, for it was dimmer, estimated at southwest of the MLVP, but he was convinced it was no car; when he told me how long he observed that light, I too was convinced it was no car headlight on a highway: two and a half hours. It reminded him of the first two lights except that it was either more red or reddish more often. It twinkled much more than any star and moved back-and-forth and up-and-down.

James later told me that those first two sightings (two lights, then another one, more distant) he believes were over two separate mountain ranges.

At 5:52 a.m. several lights appeared where the first two had been. About seven to ten of them lit up and went out. Occasionally some would flash much brighter. At 6:30 a.m. he saw on-off activity, with three to five of the lights being active. By 7:15 a.m. the distant light (2.5 hours) was gone.

A few days later, having made his boat-delivery, James arrived in Long Beach, California, delighting me with his account of *Marfa Lights*. Anxious to know if he had seen living pterosaurs, he asked my opinion; after consideration, I told him that those lights were more than likely made by flying creatures similar to the *ropen*: more than a 50% chance that he had seen the glow of living pterosaurs (not likely owls). Without more information about *Marfa Lights*, however, I could say no more.

James spent several days in Long Beach (working on the engine of his old Mercedes), asking me about the eyewitness reports I have received from around the world. He was especially interested in which American *ghost lights* were probably barn owls and which were probably pterosaurs, for he was determined to organize a successful expedition to capture a living pterosaur in North America. He impressed me with his organization.

His account of the strange lights of Marfa got me thinking. Some accounts, not quite like James's observations, involve "dancing" behavior. But if the lights are made by *ropen*-like animals, why would they move like that? Of course *ropens* in Texas might be hunting bats, but how could dancing help them catch bats? Insects! Of course lights attract insects. After two *ropens* have glowed in one area long enough to concentrate insects, they separate for awhile to allow the bats to feel safe in catching those insects. Soon the *ropens* return to catch the bats.

After visiting me in Long Beach, my friend James returned to Tennessee. Unfortunately, business challenges soon forced him to put off plans for a living-pterosaur expedition late in 2010. We still keep in touch.

Another James, Mr. Bunnell the scientist, has lived around Marfa, Texas, for much of his life. In his youth, he had assumed that somebody had already done the research and had explained what caused *Marfa Lights*, for people had seen them for countless years; how surprising when he found that nobody had come up with a convincing explanation! (James Bunnell, apparently, knew nothing about *ropens* in New Guinea; he considered only *Marfa Lights* interpretations involving light-sources non-living. I communicated with him by emails, early in 2010.) He has analyzed many factors involving observations of the mysterious lights, proving himself one of the world's leading experts, in my opinion.

Mr. Bunnell was not the first *Marfa Lights* investigator I questioned. Ed Hendricks, of Southern California, I interviewed by phone, in March of 2010. Like Bunnell, he had studied the phenomena scientifically while considering only interpretations involving light-sources non-living. After his initial rejection of the possibility of bioluminescence, I avoided that issue, listening to him instead of talking; I learned much.

Hendricks believes, but is not 100% sure, that the truly mysterious lights of Marfa are similar to ball lightning or to atmospheric lights related to the *aurora borealis* (*northern lights*). He admitted to me that *Marfa Lights* last much longer than ball lightning and are seen in all kinds of weather (discounting ball lightning), and he told me what he himself had seen, near the MLVP, unwittingly suggesting a bioluminescent creature.

Near the MLVP, Hendricks saw a light come down and move about in the nearby bushes, like an animal would. In the morning, he searched those bushes but found nothing. I suspect that Hendricks had witnessed a *ropen*-like nocturnal flying predator that was chasing a *Big Brown Bat*. (See, in the appendix, "Living Nightmare: Attack in the Dead of Winter.")

In March of 2010, I read Bunnell's book, *Hunting Marfa Lights*. From those 315 pages I learned much: Marfa *ML's* (*mystery lights*) he divides into several types; Not all of them suggest *ropen*-bioluminescence, but in my opinion some of them do. Many strange lights can be explained as common phenomena: night mirages (especially with car headlights), meteors, *sprites* (high-altitude lightning), train lights, satellites, low-flying military aircraft, a USAF radar blimp (monitoring traffic from Mexico into the U.S.), ranch house lights, and even fireworks (around July 4th and January 1st). But one general type caught my attention: "CE."

Suggesting "chemical or combustion-like properties with electro-magnetic attributes—those, of four subtypes, are CE *ML's*. Subtype III struck me.

Both II and III subtypes involve "balls of light that turn on and off and sometimes multiply," but II is titled "stationary" and III, "traveling." The possibility of *ropen*-like creatures became obvious when I read, "they travel cross-country above desert foliage and below background mesas."

How long the path to writing *Hunting Marfa Lights*! (Bunnell had written two related books before HML.) Perhaps the greatest challenge at first was distance from observer to object: Large areas of private property—that's where the mysterious lights usually appear, and he needed a closer look. Land owners were naturally suspicious of strangers, but Bunnell was a local man and he soon became friends with some local cattle ranchers. Having gained their trust, he set up automatic cameras on the plain where *Marfa Lights* are more common, but it was no simple operation: Installations and observations have taken years. Problems included how to obtain power supply for automatic cameras and, when solar panels were chosen, how to prevent cattle from using solar panels for back scratchers.

Early in 2003, one rancher was kind enough to allow Bunnell to set up a camera on the roof of one of his buildings. That first camera station was named "Roofus," and it would soon prove the value of its lofty location.

On February 19th, it recorded time-exposed photographs of a light flying west; the wind may have died off by 8:20 p.m., but it was coming from another direction. The light resembled rapid on-off states of chemical combustion: starting to burn, almost dying off, then starting up again, with occasional outbursts of greater intensity. Nothing in Bunnell's description of this event contradicted what might be expected of a *ropen*-like flying creature periodically secreting something that causes extreme bioluminescence. Of course the degree of brightness is extraordinary, but true science allows for the possibility of discoveries extraordinary.

Two other camera stations were eventually installed on the plain, allowing triangulation to determine where any particular *mystery lights* originated.

On May 7th and 8th, 2003, extraordinary events were photographed. On the first night, lights appeared between 9:00 and 10:40. The first light was too brief for Bunnell to photograph, but two more appeared at about the same location. I was intrigued at Bunnell's description of how those two lights behaved, for it seemed consistent with my hypothesis that *Marfa Lights* are made by flying predators with extreme bioluminescence, like the *ropen* of the southwest Pacific but used for a different purpose: to attract insects that attract the *Big Brown Bat*.

The May 7th pair of lights remained together for only a short time; the one on the right moved off to the right and traveled for awhile. The traveling light was joined by another that followed it. Those two continued to the right for awhile but eventually reversed course, going back toward the stationary light that was not completely still: That first light was "dancing." The flying lights went out before reaching the dancing light.

According to Bunnell's notes, sunset on May 7th was at 8:36 p.m.; there was no wind and the temperature was "about 70 degrees F." I wonder: Could it have been warm enough at 10:40 p.m. for insects to be flying around? I believe so. The dancing light would have attracted insects to that general location, perhaps enough for bats to come near, not near enough to be caught by the dancing *ropen*, but not far off, for hunger drives us to take chances. But the other two *ropens*, the ones streaking back to that location, were also driven by hunger, and they were not heading in that direction by chance. That would explain why the lights seen by my friend James, late in February of 2010, behaved differently: It was too cold for insects.

So why did the two lights of May 7th go out before reaching the original location? Think about it. Several bats are grabbing a few insects while also keeping track of a nearby dancing, glowing bat-eater. Is it really a free lunch? The other two bat-eaters, having turned off their glow, are streaking into that area at high speed, relying on the dancing bat-eater to hold the attention of the bats. Who survives? Some bats, some *ropens*, some insects.

In March of 2010, I sent an email to the author, giving details about my friend's recent sighting in Marfa, but withholding any reference to pterosaurs. He soon replied, thanking me and telling me about similar lights in Italy, where they are said to be precursors of earthquakes.

In my second email to Bunnell, I got to the point (pterosaurs); but my wording, here quoted, requires an explanation. I had learned from the last page of his book that he is a space-rocket engineer, having been a member of all the manned Apollo launches (1968-1973), including those involving astronauts walking on the moon and returning safely to earth.

"Until I read your book, 'Hunting Marfa Lights,' much of what I knew about these ML I had learned from speaking with Edson Hendricks . . . Although my exposure to these ML is recent, I have interviewed many eyewitnesses of mysterious lights in Papua New Guinea, especially during my 2004 expedition to Umboi Island, PNG. What I share with you may seem to ask stretching the imagination too much; but I have learned what I have from both indirect accounts and direct interviews with eyewitnesses, and the results do add up.

"My interpretation of the Subtype III traveling ML of the Marfa area is not 100% sure to me; I would put my assurity [sic] of my interpretation at 75%+. Nevertheless, many similarities between *Marfa Lights* and the lights that I have studied seem too many to ignore, strange as the ultimate interpretation appears to be; the overall hypothesis answers many questions about the behaviors of the ML-III in southwest Texas.

"I do not doubt that many forces in the earth, air, and space can cause mysterious lights of varous [sic] kinds. But I doubt that they will create anything like the horizontally-flying lights around Marfa. There is, however, an explanation that addresses those seemingly strange movements.

"Loss of glow and re-ignition during flight [subtitle in the email]

"First, please consider one idea about these traveling Marfa Lights, ML-III. A simple explanation for their apparent tendency to lose energy during flight is this: A physical object is losing energy during flight. Please excuse me if this seems rude to mention to a rocket expert. The mystery is not in this simple concept, of course; it is this: What object would appear to be a natural part of this area of Texas, yet resemble so much a man-made rocket in the way that it seems to run out of fuel (although for only a short while) during flight. [?]

"Regarding the drop of glowing substance that appeared to be all that was left of one of the ML-III, I suggest that this was only a remnant of the fuel itself. It was not the object that uses and produces the fuel, nor is this fuel used for propulsion. Perhaps "fuel" is not the word; this is something that glows, but dissolves or dissiptes [sic] over time. It must be replentished [sic]. But the substance that glows is only a part of what is flying.

"Complex object [second subtitle of email]

"Next, please consider the possibility that the object holding this fuel is far more complex than the fuel itself. I don't mean anything like a space craft; any civilization intelligent enough to visit our planet would have no reason to fly over the bushes south of Marfa for years beyond number. Bushes are not that interesting. No, the ML-III are too-closely connected to the terrain of southwest Texas, I believe. They are very much of this earth. I believe that you and other investigators have a good sense of this and that you are correct in connecting the lights with this earth. No ET's here.

"Basic purpose of the aerobatic behavior [third subtitle of email]

"Next, let's reduce the aerobatics to a simpler form, one that is familiar. Compress the movements of Type-III into purely horizontal form (they seem mostly horizontal anyway). Take those motions and put them onto the ground, but not in Texas: to a savannah in Africa. Consider the speed of 150-200 m.p.h. to be a mistake; assume the speed is about half that (75 m.p.h.). Now take away the glow, reduce the speed a bit more, and consider this: What could make those movements? Of course, a group of large predators, hunting. The big cats of Africa start their charge as a group, dividing up at first, coming back together later. Of course cheetahs neither glow nor fly; but they move around, over many days, to follow herds of prey, and they return to old territory, perhaps after many days absence.

"Why are ML-III not usually seen for many nights in a row? Why are they absent for so many nights in a row? Why do they keep coming back after a few weeks of absence? This is exactly what we would expect of large predators that cover large areas. Could Marfa Lights actually be only a small part of the big picture? I suspect that similar lights might be seen in other areas of southwest Texas and in bordering areas of Mexico. I believe that some of these are the same individuals that appear near Marfa. I know that verifying this could be an enormous undertaking, comparing when the ML-III are seen in various areas by monitoring further south. But it is possible.

"Contributions of Hendricks [fourth subtitle of email]

"I learned several things from Edson Hendricks, although he did not grab hold of my 'animal' idea during our phone conversation. (I know my interpretation appears incredible.) Instead of trying to convince him of large bioluminescent flying predators, I allowed him to tell me his experiences.

"Ed noticed that the overall formation of flying lights that he observed were moving as a whole. The movement of the center of the formation (I believe that's how he put it) seems to me consistent with a group of large predators moving across an area slowing, while hunting. He also saw one of these lights fly close to the MLVP one night, scurrying around in some bushes 'like an animal.' What if it actually was an animal? How wonderful! But I did not press that point with Ed. I know my interpretation seems almost impossible, and it was my turn to learn, not to teach.

"Explanation for spiraling behavior [fifth subtitle of email]

"Why would one light spiral up just before an apparently imminent head-on collision with another flying light? If the lights had nothing to do with living organisms they could either be attractive to each other or repulsive to each other, but not both attractive and repulsive at the same time. Whatever had flown up to avoid those two predators, it was followed by one spiraling pursuer. I submit that no non-living explanation can come close to the reasonableness of this interpretation.

"Two non-living balls of plasma (or any other non-living balls) will never, without intelligent direction, separate and fly apart from some distance, both change course by 180 degrees, and fly back towards each other before one of them spirals up and away, avoiding a collision. Two out of those three activities would be hard to imagine with inanimate objects; all three, never."

"Big Brown Bats and apparent predation [sixth subtitle of email]

"*Big Brown Bats* are common in Southern Texas, I believe. (What may be hunting them appears anything but common.) If my information is correct, this bat hibernates, in many instances, in the same areas where it hunts insects in warmer weather. The year-round life of this bat may be critical; this bat supplies food for large flying predators. The prey of this bat (insects) seems critical to why its predator glows. But it is only one of the reasons why the larger flying creatures glow. Nevertheless, the bat-connection hypothesis seems worth considering.

"Consider the simplest variation of the splitting-rejoining activity of two ML-III. (If I am correct in this, it will be far more common in warmer weather than in the dead of winter.) Let's label the large bioluminescent flying predator LBFP. One has been glowing while hovering over bats that are hunting insects. A second LBFP joins the first one, turning on its glow in a flash ignition. By about this time, flying insects are beginning to congregate closer to this area. The two LBFP then separate, giving distant humans the impression that one light has divided into two. After leaving the area in opposite directions, a few bats wander into the area now devoid of threatening LBFP, for that is where there are more insects. Soon, however, the two LBFP both change course by 180 degrees and converge on the bats. One bat may avoid one LBFP while being caught by the other LBFP.

"**That's all for now** [seventh and last subtitle of email]

"I agree with you, James, that owls are not the answer. Even the largest most nimble barn owls can never produce the incredible displays that are being observed. They are too slow of wing and of mind and they lack whatever it takes to produce the shocking brilliance of those ML-III lights. Nevertheless, larger predators appear to be the most reasonable answer, as shocking as that may be. More later."

Bunnell replied cordially, and showed appreciation for some of my reasoning, but seemed unprepared for the strange interpretation I offered. He concluded with, "Your concept, interesting as it may be, does not fit my collected observations." I was disappointed, at first, for the reasoning behind his rejection of my hypothesis appeared sound.

But the more I examined his objections, the more I realized that they were objections to the specific hunting behavior that I offered to him. The overall concept of bioluminescent predators does not, in my view, contradict his observations, at least not in the specifics he offered.

Bunnell pointed out that my idea related to the horizontally moving lights (ML-III's) but "ML-IIs are also common and sometimes transition into the ML-IIIs. . . . I have observed ML-IIs stay in one spot, pulsing on and off for as much as seven hours." Yes, I admit that does seems to shoot down the hypothesis I offered to him. I thought about it a little and realized that there is an explanation: What if one of the nocturnal predators were to act alone to try to catch a bat? Weather permitting, would it not sit in a bush and glow on and off for hours, attracting insects and, eventually, a bat? So that point does not shoot down "glowing predator."

Another point by Bunnell appeared to shoot down any possibility of a biological interpretation. He told me of one ML-II that grew to an enormous size. It lit up clouds "to an extent similar to the amount of cloud illumination caused by the city of Alpine when viewed from the same distance with overhead clouds at a similar height." It lasted three hours without going anywhere. He estimated that the actual size was probably more than one hundred meters in diameter.

I was stumped . . . for awhile. That extraordinary light display on June 3, 2005, did seem hard to explain with bioluminescent creatures, even with a giant *ropen*. That kind of sighting, I suspect, is rare; but what else would be rare, with large bioluminescent predators? Would not a court-ship ritual be rare, one that involved many *ropens* competing for mates? How would they compete? Why not glow as brightly as you can for as long as possible? How large a circle might a number of them make, as they sat and glowed? I suppose such a circle might be more than a hundred meters in diameter.

After Bunnell photographed lights on May 8, 2003, he said that their "behavior was becoming increasingly complex and ever more mysterious." The end-point of one flying light was eleven miles from start-point, flown in eighteen minutes, so it would have been flying at least thirty-seven miles per hour: a perfectly believable speed for a *ropen*.

Large flying predators that eat bats—that idea is not so revolutionary. Living pterosaurs and extremely brilliant bioluminescent—that's different, apparently too different for the comfort of many Americans. Yet it seems to fit at least some of the lights observed around Marfa, Texas.

Another investigator grew up in that part of Texas (I don't know his name; I read of his experiences through an online forum). In the area of the Chinati mountains he once observed "balls of light sitting in a chico bush." On another occasion he saw a light that "moved straight up a cliff face and then rested on top of the mountain." At least some of the lights he had seen changed color dramatically (*ropen* lights in Papua New Guinea are said to be of various colors). Like other investigators, he has searched not only for lights but for a non-living explanation for them. I don't know what would be more natural, however, for a nocturnal flying predator, than to sit in a chico bush or fly up a cliff face to rest on a mountain top. I do know how revolutionary "bioluminescent flying predator" appears in light of the extraordinary brilliance of that light.

Without sightings of apparent living pterosaurs in Texas, and without reports of brilliantly glowing *ropens* in the southwest Pacific, I would hesitate speculating about bioluminescent flying predators near Marfa. I understand how difficult it must be for scientists who have never been exposed to those human experiences, how hard to consider the revolutionary idea I suggest. Yet how easy it is to underestimate the magnificent potential of life! And how wonderful it will be to discover a revolutionary new living species! Let us rise above the dust under the bushes of Marfa, and soar up through the clouds, into the sky of a new discovery.

Chapter 7
The Truth of Tall Tails

Two years after our Umboi Island expeditions of 2004, my friend, fellow *ropen* seeker Garth Guessman, told me of three eyewitnesses of *Pteranodon*-like animals on New Britain Island, east of Umboi. They had ten daylight sightings, 1989-1991, of tail-less featherless creatures that glided over a valley, deep in the island interior. Guessman gave me detailed reports of the descriptions given by these three American missionaries. The combined descriptions convinced me that those three had reported actual events; it was no hoax-collaboration. But rare be tales of no-tails.

Sightings in the United States seem to indicate at least a 4-1 ratio favoring long-tailed pterosaurs over short-tailed or no-tailed ones. Although this resembles the ratio in southwest Pacific nations, I found a limit to the usefulness of the data. The long-tailed *ropens*, here and abroad, may be mostly nocturnal, at least compared with creatures lacking long tails. If so, the populations of long-tailed *ropens* may dominate *Pterodactyloid*-like populations even more. Of course, with limited data and difficulties observing creatures in the dark, that is speculative.

Regardless, long tails deserve a long look, especially when we consider worldwide legends of long-tailed flying dragons or "flying snakes."

David Woetzel, another fellow *ropen*-seeker, after the 2004 expeditions, wrote "The Fiery Flying Serpent" (*Creation Research Society Quarterly*, March, 2006). But Woetzel mentions more than quotations from Isaiah and detailed opinions of Bible scholars. He compares Biblical references (to "flying serpents,") with accounts of ancient historians: Herodotus and Josephus. And he mentions the account of the ancient Assyrian monarch Esarhaddon, who saw "yellow flying snakes" in the desert. There seem to be many ancient accounts of what were once called "flying snakes."

Do we have only cryptozoological evidence for "flying snakes," ancient or not? No. A *Rhamphorhynchoid* pterosaur, with a somewhat long neck and very long tail, could have been anciently labeled a "flying snake," and we do have fossil evidence for *Rhamphorhynchoids*: significant evidence.

Anciently, "flying serpents" in northern Africa and Saudi Arabia were said to be numerous. If modern *Rhamphorhynchoids*, rare-and-nocturnal or not, are seen occasionally around the world, we should have other records of the creatures within the past few centuries, and according to Woetzel's paper we do have other records.

He quoted a passage from a book by Marie Trevelyan (1909), who interviewed an old man who remembered "winged serpents" that lived in the mid-1800's around Penllyne Castle, Glamorgan, Wales.

I quote part of Woetzel's quotation of the book:

"The woods around Penllyne Castle, Glamorgan, had . . . . winged serpents . . . An aged inhabitant of Penllyne, who died a few years ago . . . said it was 'no old story,' invented to 'frighten children,' but a real fact. His father and uncles had killed some of them, for they were 'as bad as foxes for poultry.' This old man attributed the extinction of winged serpents to the fact that they were 'terrors in the farmyards and coverts.'"

If this old story from a village in Wales were an isolated account unrelated to any other story, it could be dismissed; but accounts come from other areas of Wales. From what I've read, the word "gwiber" (which now refers to *venomous snakes) originally meant "winged snake;" *gwibers*, only a few generations ago, were thought to be real animals. (And *venomous bites caused the deaths of Israelites, according to the account of Moses.)

Winged snakes or pterosaur-like animals were hardly restricted to Wales. Other parts of Europe had similar creatures, and dragon legends in general abound all over the world. This abundance of dragon legends, worldwide, is not denied by those who assert that those legends must all be completely fictional. Dragon stories have been popular worldwide, regardless of the potential truth and fiction in details in particular stories.

Woetzel's paper includes an account recorded by seventeenth-century writer, Athanasius Kircher; the eyewitness was Chistopher Schorerum:

"On a warm summer night in 1619 . . . I saw a shining dragon of great size in front of Mt. Pilatus [Switzerland] . . . [flying] rapidly . . . with a long tail, a long neck, a reptile's head . . . [the creature] scatters sparks."

What about the responses of twenty-first-century critics? I will not quote the libels of a critic who has throw together "stupid" and "lies" to create the URL-name for web pages about me and my associates. But since one page refers to both Penllyne Castle and Mt. Pilatus, the reasoning of that critic now deserves a response.

The Penllyne (or Penllin) Castle creatures are labeled "winged serpents" in the Trevelyan book. The critic insists on the label "amphiptere" (also spelled "amphithere"), which refers to legends of a dragon that had wings. I don't recall any mention of "amphiptere" in any of Woetzel's writings, so why mention that label? Perhaps the critic uses that word because most old ideas include an absence of legs on that dragon.

Why insist on technical accuracy of certain details in ancient descriptions of old legends? My associates and I do not believe that everything written anciently about dragons must be either completely accurate or completely fictional. Why should ancient labels be as technically accurate as modern scientific labels? Nineteenth-century farmers in Wales could have labeled a small creature "winged serpent" even though it had small *Rhamphorhynchoid* feet. When the creatures were observed, would they not be flying with legs folded up to their bodies, hardly noticeable legs?

And why not consider the possibility that "amphiptere" refers to a real animal that was seen under less-than-ideal conditions, concealing real legs? Perhaps similar animals, or the same ones, that were seen with legs were more often labeled "gwiber." I suspect that the critic fails to consider that possibility because it would make the old animals too pterosaur-like.

We need to remember that these eyewitnesses in centuries past were not a group of organized scientists who collected data, analyzed it, then agreed on labeling and classifying similar animals of different species; they were mostly common folk who saw, under imperfect observing conditions, animals that they called by the old names available at the time.

The Trevelyan book mentions that the winged serpents were sometimes "coiled in repose." The critic says that "pterosaurs completely lack . . . coiling bodies." Wait a minute. What if that eyewitness was referring to wings? *Rhamphorhynchoid* pterosaur fossils are frozen in stone, but when they were living and reposed they would have "coiled" up wings, right? I suspect that this critic's thinking is frozen on discrediting Woetzel.

The book also mentions that "some of them had crests sparkling with all the colors of the rainbow." The critic admits that some pterosaurs had head crests, but declares that "no one really knows what colored [sic] the pterosaurs were." But the declaration that "none of the crests . . . sparkle like jewels" (a declaration of the critic) rings dogmatic to me. How can anyone know that no pterosaur had anything like that? We have only a relatively few fossils, rather deteriorated. The critic seems to rely on two assumptions: No pterosaur fossil could be from an animal that had sparkled, and no pterosaur that did not leave a fossil sparkled; I challenge those assumptions of that presumptuous critic.

Regarding the 1619 sighting near Mt. Pilatus, the critic declares that "no pterosaur ever glow [sic], sparkle . . ." but gives nothing to back up that declaration. Many details about extraordinary or supernatural aspects of dragon lore—those are what the critic emphasizes. But Woetzel and I do not declare that all details in dragon tales are nonfictional; we suggest that certain details in some accounts do suggest that *Rhamphorhynchoid* pterosaurs were observed in previous centuries, and we maintain that the overall historical evidence supports the existence, in human times, of live bioluminescent *Rhamphorhynchoid* pterosaurs, regardless of the irrelevant errors that seem to taint those old records. How many old records are imperfect yet useful! And why be offended at "dragon" in those old records?

Woetzel and I have relied on more than old stories. Along with several other Americans, we have used personal funds to explore a remote tropical wilderness where villagers regularly see glowing flying creatures. If dragons were only fictions of the past, what was the strange glowing form Woetzel saw flying to Mount Tolo, the same area where native eyewitnesses had seen giant long-tailed creatures flying (in separate sightings)? And if Woetzel tells "lies" about live dragons, why, after many days in the jungle, did he admit that he saw no form or features of a dragon?

The question I put to those who insist on non-pterosaur interpretations is this: "Since we know, from fossils, that pterosaurs existed, why not consider the possibility that some still live?" Those who are free from the constraints of the ancient-extinction dogma enjoy the freedom to consider dragon tales objectively; those who have surrendered to the indoctrination that certain general types must be extinct—those persons may feel constrained to repeat the propaganda that prohibits "dragon" from referring to any real animal like a living dinosaur or pterosaur.

The point? Modern science textbooks should not be used like Bibles or pseudo-religious creed-books. Real science progresses, and progress means change, including correcting old mistakes.

Now to the next point: Long-tailed pterosaurs, (glowing, bioluminescent, sparkling, or dull) are not misidentified bats; but there is a connection.

Chapter 8

The Bat Connection

When I began investigating living-pterosaur reports, a common explanation was "fruit bats," not that Hodgkinson's description of a tail "at least 10-15 feet long" could suggest any *flying fox* bat; but critics habitually ignore details, conveniently generalizing. The critics who've tried to dismiss the reports with "flying fox" take only one perspective: that of Western visitors to Papua New Guinea who can be shocked at those bats; natives living with fruit bats, however, also see giant long-tailed flying creatures. So why ignore all reports of apparent *Rhamphorhynchoid* pterosaurs?

Mind you, that bat conjecture is only theoretical: I've encountered no eyewitness who described a fruit bat while calling it a pterosaur, and I have encountered many eyewitnesses, many indeed. But the bat explanation sounds reasonable to specifically-ignorant Westerners who've personally encountered neither an apparent pterosaur nor an eyewitness of one.

Actually, critics generally use this criticism as one choice in a pot luck: Fruit-bat misidentification is one dish, but you might prefer a hoax hot dog or, if you're very hungry, an anti-extremist-cryptozoologist-apologist pie. Eat whatever you like, as long as it satisfies your appetite and keeps you from hungering for some strange discovery that contradicts tradition. But personally I'm especially repulsed by concoctions with ingredients of lies-of-eyewitnesses, or insanity-of-investigators, including me. Long experience with the eyewitnesses reveals their honesty.

Nevertheless, I later found a bat connection. Some of the apparent living *Rhamphorhynchoids* appear to have a relationship with some bats, and it relates not to any family tree: Bats are truly part of the pot luck.

In mid-2007, at the secret location in North America (mentioned at the beginning of Chapter 5), many bats were seen flying where flying lights were common. The bats appeared more numerous than the flying lights, and investigators were sure of at least two kinds of nocturnal fliers. Since the lights are seen throughout the year, by the local land owner, I pondered why *ropen*-like creatures would be flashing so regularly. Catching-bats jumped out at me, far ahead of a mating-ritual explanation; my associates, however, ahead of me, had already thought of that: *ropen*-eating bats.

Let us now step back from this frenzy of lights that shoot through flight paths of bats. My investigations have found nothing to disprove the idea that some unidentified species of bat may have a bioluminescence not yet acknowledged by science, so these *ropen*-like lights at this location can do little in themselves to prove extant pterosaurs; nevertheless, just as some flying lights around the world coalesce, forming part of a bigger pattern, some flights of *ropens* merge with flights of bats, forming a relationship.

Whether running on land, or swimming in water, or flying through air, many little guys are hunted and eaten by a few big guys. What allows predator to catch prey? Whether with greater speed, or with greater team work, or with greater intelligence, predators must use an advantage. And whatever elevates the predator above the prey will also make it appear different, to some degree. Of course a careless glance may not reveal any difference between a shark and the fish it eats. Falcons and sparrows are small birds; ant lions and ants are small insects. I know some exceptions: a few strange mammals eat only ants, and a few large spiders eat small birds; nevertheless, many differences are subtle, allowing predators to run or swim or fly alongside prey. The point is that there are differences.

Mammals and birds have few similarities. An exception is the Leopard Seal swimming after the Emperor Penguin, resembling a big fish swimming after a small fish; this predator-prey relationship involves a general similarity related to swimming. To a biologist, bats and pterosaurs have only limited similarity, most obviously featherless-flying. But if they lived together, flying at night, could there be a predator-prey relationship?

I know a friend of a missionary in the Congo. In one area, pterosaur-like animals are known by the natives, according to the missionary, and he himself believes he saw one swoop down on a tree full of fruit bats, causing the bats to scatter in all directions. His limited view limits evidential value for pterosaurs, but it proves bats are tasty to something that flies.

More than 1000 species of bats are spread across our planet. Most of them are small-to-medium sized, compared with birds. The smaller birds are sometimes hunted by larger ones; what about bats? Some of the flying lights are said to fly faster than bats: a potential predator-advantage; there is probably more to it than that. But there is circumstantial evidence that at least some *ropen*-like flying lights in the U.S. may involve catching bats. Some of my associates have searched night skies where both the lights and bats are common, especially bats. If I were a hungry *ropen*, built for the night, flying beyond any tropical reef, bat-banquet would jump out at me.

Chapter 9

Belief in Live Pterosaurs

Why believe in live pterosaurs? I'll explain how I came to believe. By about early 2003, I had heard of a few eyewitness reports from around the world. I got in touch with Carl Baugh and Paul Nation, of Texas, whose interviews of natives of Papua New Guinea, over several years, were videotaped. After watching the videos, I began to believe in the possibility of live pterosaurs, and this led to my interviewing, by emails in 2004, two Australian citizens and one American World War II veteran, whose encounters with giant long-tailed flying creatures eventually convinced me that *Rhamphorhynchoid* pterosaurs live in the southwest Pacific. In late 2004, I traveled to Umboi Island, Papua New Guinea, and interviewed, face-to-face, many natives whose testimonies confirmed my belief.

But a pterosaur I never saw. Even the flying *ropen*-light, seen by hundreds of Umboi Islanders as often as once a month—that more common phenomenon escaped my view. (One night, Luke, my interpreter, did see the light . . . one hour after I had fallen asleep.) Still, I returned home convinced the *ropen* was real. So how are we convinced of what we never saw?

First, is it true that "seeing is believing?" To the point, must we experience a thing personally before believing it exists? Human knowledge includes experiences acquired indirectly: We belief what we're told, at least sometimes, otherwise we'd be hermits, each ignorant of everything except what each experiences directly, without need for language, without books.

C. S. Lewis, and other deep thinkers, understood that belief can allow us to see. Belief, I believe, normally manifests itself more in what we bring to a personal experience than in what we take from it, unless we're in diapers. Lewis observed, "Experience proves this, or that, or nothing, according to the preconceptions we bring to it." Let's look deeper, for a worthy belief can enlighten us; on the other hand, an unworthy belief can blind us.

Must we believe what we see? I've noticed that when two eyewitnesses together observe an apparent pterosaur, sometimes only one will believe what both of them see. Duane Hodgkinson's army buddy stood next to him when the giant creature ran to their left, flapping its wings and then taking off into the air. Hodgkinson concluded that the long-tailed creature with a prominent head crest was a "pterodactyl." His buddy thought that was impossible. "But we saw it" was countered with, "No, we didn't."

So what did Hodgkinson's buddy bring to their experience? He'd been a college biology student; he must have brought those teachings with him into that jungle clearing near Finschhafen, New Guinea. He saw what his less-educated buddy saw, but he allowed traditional teachings to control his thoughts to the point that he denied part of his experience.

What did Hodgkinson bring to their experience? He had lived most of his teenage years on a farm in Ohio, learning about farm animals by observing them. In 1944, he was assigned to be a weather observer for the artillery. He learned by observation, not that he was uneducated: He completed plane-mechanics training, later becoming a certified flight instructor. The point? He brought open-mindedness into that jungle clearing.

That is not to say that college biology courses teach close-mindedness. It seems that the marvelous twentieth-century discoveries in biology should encourage students to be open to discovery. But open-minded students may unknowingly adopt the philosophy of the professors, and part of a popular philosophy is that some species need to become extinct for other species to arise. If true, that would suggest the necessity of dinosaur and pterosaur extinction, that it should be. Nevertheless, I smell dogma.

Of course, one could propose that the farm boy had a faulty belief. But did Hodgkinson see a creature with a wingspan of a Piper Tri-Pacer airplane because he believed in live pterosaurs? No. To him, a "pterodactyl" was something he saw only in a newspaper comic strip. In fact, when he first noticed something flapping its wings, he assumed it was a bird. But he quickly became a believer by the time the creature had turned in flight and flew back over the jungle clearing, giving another clear view of itself.

Both Americans, before their experience, assumed universal pterosaur extinction, but the biology student apparently held it dogmatically. That soldier was probably so firmly entrenched in the extinction dogma, so rigidly trained to obey its command, that he rebelled against his personal experience with a giant *Rhamphorhynchoid* pterosaur. It was Hodgkinson who accepted the truth of what both of them experienced.

Now consider the couple in the California desert. Both of them recognized the appearance of a pterosaur, but one of them "looked in the binoculars and said it looked like one but it had to be a kite or something because they [pterosaurs] were extinct." Notwithstanding that belief, the man's kite-explanation did not hold up at the sun's going down: He was enlightened enough (or nervous enough) to spend the night in a different canyon.

Now compare the daylight desert experience with the comfort of a front porch in Florida: Two men are spending part of the night talking. Instead of one giant no-tailed pterosaur gliding in the distance, two small long-tailed pterosaurs flap nearby. One man says, "Was that what I think it was?" The other says, "naa, it had to be something else." Note the similarity.

In each of these three sightings, two eyewitnesses saw the same thing, but one accepted what was seen. (Of course the descriptions differ, but the creatures were in different places, in different environments; why should they be the same species? The similarity of these three sightings causes me to ponder differences between humans more than differences between pterosaur species.) Three of the six eyewitnesses appear to have perceived what their doubting companions perceived, but they came to believe the obvious meaning: a live pterosaur.

Why do some eyewitnesses disbelieve what they see? First consider what they admit about their experiences. In a jungle clearing, a soldier declares that he did not see a pterodactyl; in a desert, it "had to be a kite or something;" near a front porch, "it had to be something else." Each admits observing something, but each maintains that he should not have seen that something. The problem is in a dogmatic belief: that among many species of pterosaurs that have once lived, not one species survived extinction.

Now compare those reactions to those of natives in Papua New Guinea. My experience interviewing natives and reviewing interviews done by other explorers—that suggests it's easier to catch a giant *ropen* in a fishing net than to find a native eyewitness who disbelieves personal experience because of what American professors assume. Eyewitnesses in a culture that dogmatically teaches pterosaur extinction—they sometimes have problems dealing with an experience that they feel should not have been experienced; native eyewitnesses in New Guinea have no problem.

But how can "prehistoric" pterosaurs fly in the twenty-first century? Why would anyone believe that mysterious flying lights witnessed in some parts of the world are giant bioluminescent pterosaurs? And what are the relationships between modern live pterosaurs, science, religion, Western culture, and philosophy? These questions I've tried to answer in my book

Searching for Ropens (SFR). Two years after writing the second edition of that book, while I was writing the first edition of this book, I was about to set aside issues that had already been examined; I soon realized that they could not be ignored here, for questions about the existence of modern pterosaurs are inseparably connected to origin philosophies. So consider now a few points about extinction concepts, but for the deeper issues of religion and science see, in the appendix, "Philosophy at the foundation."

What has a beak and a long tail, and flies with no feathers? . . . Some would reply, "Living or extinct?" But why not just answer that question? Of course it is a *Rhamphorhynchoid* (long-tailed) pterosaur, called by many non-scientists "pterodactyl," a layman's term for any reptilian-like "pre-historic" featherless flying creature. The point? What's wrong with simply accepting an eyewitness report of a long-tailed featherless flying creature? Why believe that all pterosaur species must be extinct? Without the idea of universal *Rhamphorhynchoid* extinction, we conclude that the eyewitness saw a pterosaur. Non-extinction, as an alternative, now appears.

Where did we get the idea of pterosaur extinction? Early discoverers of pterosaur fossils had no knowledge of living pterosaurs; they assumed they were looking at the remains of extinct creatures, and that assumption has been magnified for two centuries. I believe that the idea was cemented into Western thought when Darwin's General Theory of Evolution became popular in the nineteenth century, but search textbooks in vain for solid scientific evidence of pterosaur extinction, for the conjecture itself is more philosophical than scientific. It is an assumption.

Now consider how a species of pterosaur could still be living. Is it really impossible? After interviewing eyewitnesses for five years, I'm convinced that pterosaurs live, even more than one species; but I understand how most Americans can be surprised or even shocked at the idea. I'm also convinced that one reason for surprise relates to culture: We are taught from kindergarten through college that dinosaurs and pterosaurs became extinct millions of years ago. Extinction is drilled into us.

This world is filled with incredible forms of life. For those ignorant of ocean life, an aquatic mammal as big as a house could be unbelievable. For those ignorant of African life, the neck of a giraffe or the nose of an elephant could be unbelievable. For those ignorant of eyewitness accounts from Papua New Guinea, it would be a featherless flying creature with a tail seven meters long. But for those Westerners raised in a culture drenched in the universal dinosaur-pterosaur-extinction axiom, "living" could be un-believable, even in a world filled with incredible forms of life.

But large bioluminescent pterosaurs living in the United States—that is shocking. It may be helpful to consider it in context: giant bioluminescent pterosaurs in Papua New Guinea. Let's consider that idea first, then look deeper at human belief, through a symbolic story.

Giant bioluminescent pterosaurs may require some faith, but not fanatical blind faith. From 1993 through 2007, expeditions in Papua New Guinea have revealed something other than baseless native superstitions. The strange flying lights have been videotaped by a few Americans and seen up close by a few natives. Video footage has been analyzed by a few experts and the natives have been interviewed. The lights could not be explained away as non-bioluminescent and the native accounts supported American and Australian eyewitness accounts. Our faith seems justified.

In *Searching for Ropens*, I explained how a broadly-popular *surface belief* differs from a belief related to personal experience. Although no biology professor has personally experienced universal extinction of pterosaurs, the teaching of that idea in developed countries appears to be universal; nevertheless, repeating "extinct" only spreads a thin layer of extinction-belief over a large area of human society, without increasing any depth.

Now consider a symbol for the belief in universal pterosaur extinction. An overnight shower falls on a huge desert dry lake, just before sunrise. Looking to the east, over that vast flatness, at sunrise what do we see? The glare on the wet surface resembles the glare on the surface of the deepest ocean. But here the sun continues to rise over moist earth, and the burning rays evaporate what first appeared to be a lake. Soon a light breeze carries away moist air. What do we see by late morning? No more glare on that dry earth. What about late afternoon? Hours of sunlight have warmed the lake bed, creating a mirage, an apparent wetness that shimmers before us.

Twice in one day that vast area of desert has appeared somewhat like a large body of water. Children who visited the area only in the early morning and late afternoon of that day could have been fooled (and why would they go to that lake at mid-day, when it should be "hot and humid?"). But an old map of that desert also misleads most city dwellers, for it gives the name of the lake but the word "dry" is carelessly absent.

How does my dry-lake story relate to belief in living pterosaurs? Those who often visit that desert need not be perplexed by mistakes, on a map or by children; those who have observed a living pterosaur need not be perplexed by mistakes, in a textbook or by inexperienced professors. The breadth of that lake gives no evidence of water depth; the popularity of extinction ideas gives no evidence of universal pterosaur-extinction.

Personal experience of those who regularly visit that desert—this proves the lake is dry, regardless of its remoteness, but the words of a few children and the mistake on the old map can lead many city dwellers to believe a falsehood (that is, assuming the desert is too remote for more than a few persons to ever visit). Regarding pterosaurs, I accuse no professor of telling a lie about extinction; but regurgitation of a falsehood, regardless of innocent ignorance, hinders the progress of human knowledge. Regular visits to a desert and regular eyewitness accounts of living pterosaurs should cause a reevaluation of old assumptions. Indeed, overall personal-experience eventually will prevail.

Mislabeling something on a map—that comes not just from my imagination. I explored Umboi Island, Papua New Guinea, in 2004, to search for the *ropen*. After I had arrived in Gomlongon Village, it seemed obvious that the small mountain to the west was *Tanglup*, for it was on the map. But Mark Kau, a local leader, told me it was not *Tanglup*; it was *Tolo*. All the natives called the mountain *Tolo*, so the conclusion was inevitable: The mistake was in the map (nevertheless, *Tanglup* is nearby). Other explorers were also corrected, later. The point? Any map that may be created with reference to that old map will multiply the mistake, and few persons visit that remote island, so that mistake may take a long time to be corrected, officially; likewise with the regurgitated nineteenth-century universal-extinction conjecture.

But there's more to this dry-lake symbolism. Why do I say "remoteness," for what desert on earth is too remote to be explored by scientists? What about the Western belief in universal pterosaur extinction? Can any group of scientists observe the extinction of even one species of animal, even when it is in "human times?" But this belief, peculiar to Western society, does not allow for even one species of pterosaur to survive, even when many other kinds of animals did survive something destructive. And what was that "something?" Whatever the destruction was (a kindergartner once told me it was a comet, but he was too young to know for sure), it was supposed to have been not thousands or tens-of-thousands or hundreds-of-thousands of years ago but many millions of years ago. How remote!

Consider the three main points of the symbolic story: an early-morning wet soil, a late-afternoon wet-appearing mirage, and a mistake on a map. Each could be mistakenly taken as evidence that supports the other two. But how do they relate to belief or disbelief in living pterosaurs? Early discoverers of pterosaur fossils had no experience with live pterosaurs; late-nineteenth century followers of Darwin found apparent justification for natural selection; twentieth century biology students were raised in a society believing pterosaurs live only in fiction or millions of years ago.

But just as close examination of the dry lake reveals lack of water depth, close examination of the universal-extinction-of-pterosaurs idea reveals lack of depth in reasoning. Personal experience of eyewitnesses should take precedence over dogma.

For those who've never personally encountered a living pterosaur, belief comes from experiencing the accounts of those who have. The strength of my own belief comes largely from the credibility of individual eyewitnesses, however, and this matter of credibility deserves attention.

So how should we judge eyewitness credibility? Here we must distinguish between individual and overall credibility. Factors that make the words of an individual eyewitness believable or unbelievable I often keep secret; revealing details could make it easy for a hoaxer to someday fool me (not that those who have previously sought to discredit me and my associates have ever examined our reasonings in detail). Factors that make the overall eyewitness reports believable, however, are practically impossible for hoaxers to exploit, for they'd need to read my mind in the future: how I will analyze the overall data. An analysis of compiled data I can reveal.

But we also need to ask the right question. I suggest using the example of the official discovery of African gorillas, beginning in the mid-nineteenth century. When the Protestant missionary Thomas S. Savage obtained bones of what we now call the "Western Gorilla," he was beginning to answer a question: "Does a large previously-unclassified primate live in Africa?" A wrong question could have been formed: "Does one species of a large previously-unclassified primate live in Africa?" (Now we know of two gorilla species.) Following that example, we can form a related question: "Does any pterosaur presently live on the earth?" The number of living species is secondary, becoming important after the official discovery of one.

With this open-ended question about pterosaurs, what about the possibility of hoaxes? Could several or many hoaxes have caused these many eyewitness accounts? A close examination discounts this idea, in several ways.

Consider descriptions of tail length. For decades, movies with "prehistoric" animals have often included flying creatures with no tails. How rare the *Rhamphorhynchoid* movie star! (*Pterodactyloids* generally have small tails, if any.) When Americans encounter the word "pterodactyl," they think of a *Pterodactyloid* more often than a long-tailed pterosaur. But why do detailed examinations of twentieth century and twenty-first century reports reveal few no-tails? I found that for those who could see the presence or absence of a tail (night sightings are often insufficient), 84% reported a tail that was long. If hoaxers played a major part, they would have described *Pterodactyloids* more than *Rhamphorhynchoids*, so the overwhelming preponderance of long-tails discredits any hoax hypothesis.

Also, one popular idea in biology is that the more-recent pterosaurs were *Pterodactyloids*, and that they were descended from *Rhamphorhynchoids*. If there were American hoaxers who were influenced more by biology textbooks than by movies, they would still have fabricated *Pterodactyloid* stories. But the reports will disprove any hypothesis of hoaxes.

Reports in the southwest Pacific indicate a preponderance of long tails, with 75% to 95% of the reports including that detail (a precise percentage would require a precise designation of which reports are credible); but almost all of those reports have been unknown to Americans until recently. Most of the eyewitnesses I've interviewed had not yet read my book; most of their sightings were before its publication. In addition, many of the web pages about living *Rhamphorhynchoids* were published online after many of the American eyewitnesses had given their reports, not before.

But what if the tail-versus-nontail ratio is just a strange deviation? Two other factors repudiate the hoax hypothesis: answers to feathers-questions and estimates of wingspans.

The feathers-answers I divided into those that seemed sure of non-feathers and those who were less sure (I rarely examine reports with positively-observed feathers; birds I leave to bird-watchers). Because actual sightings would be at various distances, under various conditions, by various eye-witnesses having various powers of observation, we have a key: Descriptions should result in a reasonable split between definitely-no-feathers and probably-no-feathers; "probably" should at least equal "definitely," if most reports are of actual sightings of pterosaurs, but if hoaxes play a major part, then "definitely" should outnumber "probably," for why would hoaxers give anyone a reason to doubt "pterosaur?"

I found that, with the eyewitnesses who had a clear-enough view to answer "feathers" questions, "probably" outnumbered "definitely" 37% to 23%, justifying honesty-credibility: far more indicative of observations of live pterosaurs than hoaxes. (See, in the appendix, "Statistics")

What about wingspan? Both nineteenth century newspaper accounts and twentieth century science fiction movies have thrilled our imaginations with giant pterosaurs. Some late-twentieth century eyewitness reports from the southwest Pacific have also involved giant pterosaurs. At least one of these would have captured the imagination of some hoaxers, if any hoaxes had caused reports of American pterosaur sightings. But the actual report-details show something different, consistent with authentic eyewitness sightings and inconsistent with hoaxes.

First, 40% of eyewitnesses give no wingspan estimate; this in itself puts the hoax explanation in doubt, for hoaxers would include wingspan, for it has caused excitement in previous reports. But that's just the beginning.

In the first edition of this book, when the samples for analysis were fewer, it looked like there was a peak of wingspans estimates: about eight to thirteen feet. Now, with a larger sampling of eyewitness reports, that peak levels off, but the conclusion of no-hoaxes remains valid.

The range of wingspan estimates is great: two feet to thirty feet; almost completely evenly spaced are those estimates, with the exception of the very largest size-estimates, which fall off slightly. Consider: 2, 4, 4, 5, 6, 7, 8, 9, 9, 10, 11, 13, 13, 15, 17, 17, 18, 20, 21, 24, 25, 25, 27, 30. How could a living pterosaur be seen with apparent wingspans so greatly and evenly spaced? Of course eyewitness errors can smooth out data, but why such a huge range? How simple the answer! Yet, how few Americans can avoid being shocked at the obvious answer! There is no single species that can appear in ways that would produce such a smooth and wide range of wingspan estimates. Neither a clever combination of hoaxes nor a single species of pterosaurs would produce those wingspan estimates; a number of species of pterosaurs, however, with estimate errors, very well could.

Am I mistaken about more than one species of living pterosaur? Could this shape of the data result from pterosaur aging: hatchlings to medium-sized juveniles to giant old *ropens*? I admit there may be some of that. But from two feet to twenty-one feet, the estimates still seem too even to come from a combination of eyewitness-error and even-growth of one species. Multiple species of pterosaurs—that makes better sense. (More on that later.)

Getting back to examining hoax possibilities, what if two kinds of hoaxers fabricated many of the sightings? If some hoaxers relied on fossils and other hoaxers relied on reports of *ropen* sightings, the wingspan estimates would have peaked twice: below seven feet and over fifteen feet. In reality, there no peak: The pattern of estimates is too smooth for hoaxes to have played any significant part.

Does a detailed examination of a report confirm the overall evidence against hoaxes? I believe so. Consider the report of MB: an apparent *Pterodacty-loid* in the desert. Hers is a less-common report that clearly indicates the lack of a tail, although she reported her sighting to me after reading my book on long-tailed *ropens*. A hoax is unlikely. My examinations of the other testimonies have also convinced me: Eyewitnesses are honest.

The combination of tail-descriptions, featherless-descriptions, and wing-span-estimates demonstrate that no combination of hoaxes caused these reports of apparent live pterosaurs in the United States. Each of these three kinds of data alone might refute the hoax hypothesis; but the combination of all three soundly proves that hoaxes played no significant part in the reports that I have accepted as reliable evidence for living pterosaurs.

But there is more. In the United States, 56% of eyewitnesses who reported a long tail also reported a head crest. On the surface, this might seem to vindicate those critics who declare that reports of living pterosaurs "com-bine" disparate characteristics of the many species; critics thus insinuate hoaxes or imaginations cause the reports. Let's take a closer look.

We have considered how those reports of long-tailed pterosaurs are less likely to be hoaxes: No group of hoaxers from across the country would contrive reports suggesting *Rhamphorhynchoids* enough to outnumber reports suggesting *Pterodactyloids*. But why would modern long-tailed pterosaurs have head crests? Those ornaments on the back and top of the head have been associated with *Pterodactyloids*, not *Rhamphorhynchoids*. There is an explanation.

Unknown to most Americans, a few fossils of *Rhamphorhynchoids* (their fossils are small) do indicate that at least one type had a head crest; also little-known, recent research indicates that at least some pterosaurs grew head crests while the creatures were maturing (they are not hatched with complete head crests). In other words, if giant long-tailed pterosaurs were living in modern times it should not be shocking for them to have head crests. Now consider the irony: What hoaxer would have thought of that?

I mentioned that hoaxes (if there were any) did not cause the accumulation of reports that I deemed reliable evidence for living pterosaurs. How do I judge an eyewitness account as reliable evidence? Not as a switch between pterosaur and non-pterosaur. Each account I crudely judge in two ways: realiability-of-experience and description-of-pterosaur. The great majority of accounts in this book I have concluded to be 1) probably-experienced reasonably close to described and 2) probably a living pterosaur rather than something else.

Not every account "probably experienced" strongly suggests pterosaurs. The screeching reported in Rancho Santa Margarita, California, one night (heard by OMF) I consider secondary evidence, not to be used to convince anyone that pterosaurs live. It may someday be useful in some research.

When I proclaim "hoaxes played no significant part in the reports that I have accepted," I refer to the overall impact of all those accounts; I do not imply that not one of them could be a hoax. Critical is the concept that all these reports form a whole because of their similarities (not that every description is very much like every other, but that similarities abound.) When many separate evidences (although each not 100% convincing in itself) all point to the same conclusion, the impact is cumulative.

Compare that approach-to-evidence with the approach of a typical critic of the investigations. When an eyewitness report is mentioned by a critic, it is dismissed as worthless because it is not 100% convincing in itself. The critic might do the same with another eyewitness report, as if no number of reports can mean anything because they contradict popular models of ancient pterosaur-extinction. Those who thus attempt to protect standard models (what they call "science") fail to understand how evidence in a court of law accumulates during a trial. To judge fairly, we must see it all and allow for the possibility that evidence may accumulate with impact.

The British paleontologist Darren Naish wrote a long online blog page, dated December 23, 2007, titled "Pterosaurs alive in, like, the modern day!" Much of it describes old hoaxes and questionable reports. None of it even mentions twenty-first century explorers or the eyewitnesses they interviewed in Papua New Guinea. Nothing is said about World War II veteran Duane Hodgkinson or the psychologist-eyewitness Brian Hennessy or the Umboi natives Gideon, Mesa, and Wesley. No credit is given to my associates, Garth Guessman and David Woetzel, who constructed detailed questionnaire forms for eyewitnesses on that remote island. No credit is given to my associate Cliff Paiva, who conducted a detailed analysis of the video footage recorded by Paul Nation (who contracted two separate infections on two of his expeditions in Papua New Guinea). No acknowledgement is given to the Australian scientist in Perth who observed and later described in detail a giant flying creature. No analysis of credible eyewitness accounts is even attempted by Naish.

He seems to have drawn a conclusion from the accounts that he chose to include: "At present there is no good reason to think that any of the accounts [note: He has chosen questionable accounts, selected, apparently, to support his case] of 'living pterosaurs' are at all relevant to the study of the real pterosaurs known from [fossils]." Note the convenient ambiguity "any of the accounts." It could mean either accounts he has mentioned or any account of a living pterosaur, including those he has ignored. Naish seems to have made a strong case on this blog page, as if the supposed evidence he has covered is the critical evidence; it is not.

The ambiguity of "any of the accounts" may lead a reader to assume that Naish has covered and discredited the important reasons that many people have believed in living pterosaurs. He has mentioned not even one of the critical eyewitness accounts that have significantly supported the recent investigations and expeditions. And he has stepped outside his expertise.

It seems to me, after going over his entire page, that Naish wants to discourage any belief in any account of a living pterosaur. He seems to have made a reasonable case in disputing the reliability of the reports that he has mentioned in detail. No scientist, however, can objectively evaluate evidence that is conveniently ignored. I do not accuse him of purposefully distorting the overall evidence, but the only other explanation for his neglect appears to be this: He has not searched for evidence of life, evidence of credible eyewitnesses, evidence that might contradict assumptions, but he confines his writings to those things that he finds easy to dismiss.

Since less-credible reports are of limited relevance in the investigation of the possibility of living pterosaurs, let us ignore Naish's many examples of questionable reports; consider the more-credible reports. They are consistent with the hypothesis that more than one species of pterosaur, rare and mostly nocturnal, live (at least for much of the year) in the United States.

How could a number of species of living pterosaurs have escaped official recognition by the scientific community? I don't imply that all species known from fossils are still living; most are probably extinct. I suggest that all species still living are at least uncommon and probably mostly nocturnal. I know of only one biology professor in the United States who has actively searched for living pterosaurs (Peter Beach); he seems to have observed one fly overhead one night. But he was searching, and very few in the scientific community have searched for living pterosaurs.

It sounds shocking, suggesting that a number of species of pterosaurs live in the United States. Yet consider the wingspan estimates: One species is too few. What about other general types of organisms. What large organism lives in many parts of the world yet is represented by only one species? We know that rats and mice differ in size more than in features, as do crows and ravens, garden snakes and gopher snakes, Blue Jays and Blue Herons. (Of course, nobody will call you "crazy" for proclaiming you once saw a Blue Heron. The shock is observed in a culture that teaches the universal extinction of all species of one general type, and you saw a pterosaur.)

But what about misidentifications? Naish's blog page offers bats and birds to explain why there are sighting reports. Like many criticisms of living pterosaur investigations, however, the misidentification explanation is offered only as a general conjecture, not about the sightings by Duane Hodgkinson, Brian Hennessy, and many other eyewitnesses. Consider details in particular reports, for that is the more scientific approach.

What did Susan Wooten see flying over Highway 20 in South Carolina? Bats and birds have been eliminated. A mechanical model gliding or falling down towards the highway before recovering to fly over tree tops (without changing its slow flapping)—that has been eliminated.

What about falling asleep at the wheel? I'm surprised that critics have overlooked that possibility. I had a friend who was once awakened by a "giant bat" that was about to collide with his windshield; fortunately, his dream forced him to wake up in time. My nephew was once awakened from sleep-driving by a herd of dinosaurs crossing the road. But both cases had one thing in common: The shock of awakening stuck in the memory, for finding that you had just been sleeping at the wheel is the shock. Susan Wooten did not awaken, she was driving awake (we need more like her in California). Besides, if she had only been dreaming, other drivers would not have pulled over to the side of the highway to gaze at her dream.

Her description and sketch suggest more than just a non-bird and a non-bat: It's obviously like the *ropen* of Papua New Guinea. (Still, there are a few differences, such as in the head crest and general head-shape. But birds and bats of Papua New Guinea differ from those in South Carolina, so why should all *ropens* be identical?) The point is that the creature flying over Highway 20, in daylight and clear visibility, where drivers were stopping, was far more like a giant *Rhamphorhynchoid* than anything else.

It might be argued that Scott Norman's flying creature with a head four feet long was a dream; after all, it was about 2:00 a.m. But he stayed up for two more hours, watching for another sighting, without any indication of any sleeping before, after, or during the one sighting. And why would another man have seen a large pterosaur-like animal in the same area but in daylight? And why would many "shooting stars" there be literally un-meteoric, changing course and even shooting up instead of falling? In that location, a number of eyewitnesses have seen *ropen*-like lights and ptero-saur-forms, so a conjecture of an individual dream counts for little.

A dream conjecture (or hallucination or delusion conjecture) also counts for little when two eyewitnesses share the same sighting of a pterosaur-like animal. The Texarkana sighting is one example: Two eyewitnesses saw the creature with a wingspan estimated at 25-30 ft., as it flew near the top of a nearby tree. Two persons do not simultaneously dream a pterosaur.

What if someone dreams of a live pterosaur? Waking up discloses it was a dream, for dreams evaporate as the reality of our wakeful life dispels the spell of imagination. Eyewitnesses, worldwide, do not report dreams.

I remember one person who called me about live pterosaurs and dinosaurs; but the incredible friendships that person had with the creatures (they were said to sleep at the foot of the bed at night) made it obvious: Pterosaurs and dinosaurs would be crazy to make friends with a human, so one of them had a problem involving imagination. But that is exceptional with those I've interviewed (humans I've interviewed): The great majority who've called or emailed me showed no sign of any detachment from reality.

On the other hand, I have often encountered critics who appear to have fixed into their imaginations the universal-pterosaur-extinction dogma. I call that "unhealthy reasoning," but don't label critics "insane," for some of them call me "crazy," so they're obviously not completely deranged.

But why do our critics fight against the eyewitness evidence? Over several years, I've noticed that those critics demand from us overwhelming physi-cal evidence of extant pterosaurs, otherwise they will refuse to believe. Why do they think that our evidence must be overwhelming? We accept no burden of proof beyond reasonable doubt, as a district attorney accepts in a criminal court trial. A civil case this resembles: My associates and I present evidence for life and challenge universal pterosaur-extinction.

Our opponents appear to assume that this universal extinction has already been proven as a scientific fact; I reply, "Nobody in the last two centuries has come up with any scientific test for extinction." Our critics' position, that extinction has been proven already—that I dispute as an unfounded assumption, notwithstanding any popularity of standard models.

Part of my role has been to give a broader perspective and to encourage giving the live-pterosaur concept a fair trial, where preponderance of evidence decides the case, and I expect my readers to judge extinction by reason and evidence or lack thereof; popularity does not create evidence.

My associates and I have been accused of being unscientific or biased in our investigations, a popular criticism. In previous chapters, we have considered the accounts of many witnesses. Let's now use mathematics to evaluate the probability that non-pterosaurs caused those accounts.

Three objections have been raised against eyewitness reliability: hoaxes, misidentification, and insanity. Consider how those possibilities apply to the witnesses who have given us their accounts.

Probability makes it easy to calculate the likelihood that separate unrelated events will all turn out the same. The probability of flipping a coin once and getting tails is 50% (0.5), but what about two flips of the coin, both tails? Just multiply: 0.5 times 0.5 equals 0.25 or 25%. Flipping the coin ten times and getting tails each time—that is unlikely: about one chance in a thousand (0.5 to the tenth power, "0.5^{10}"). Now we can see the challenge with disputing thirty-five eyewitnesses who report the same thing: Thirty-five hoaxes out of thirty-five is practically impossible, even if each report were considered doubtful (as likely a hoax as a non-hoax).

But those reports from thirty-five eyewitnesses I included in this book because of their credibility, and that included the improbability of any hoax. Remember the overall evidences against any hoax? Featherless-descriptions, long-tails, estimated-sizes—each gave solid evidence against any overall hoax. The cumulative power of these thirty-five, however, proves the case separately, independent of those other evidences against hoaxes.

Even if a critic were to throw out half of the reports from those thirty-five, assuming half were misidentifications or whatever, what could that do? We would then have seventeen more-solid eyewitnesses, enough witnesses to give any opposing trial-attorney nightmares.

Do I exaggerate? Which reports would be eliminated because of possible bird-misidentifications? The sightings involving flying creatures similar in size to birds, of course. That leaves us with giant flying creatures, some seen in clear daylight, some sightings with multiple eyewitnesses. What about giant creatures with long tails, obviously not bats? What about the absence of feathers, some creatures with teeth, obviously not birds? No, there is no adequate defense for universal extinction of all species of pterosaurs through any hypothesis combining misidentifications with hoaxes, for the eyewitnesses are credible, and the creatures, neither bats nor birds.

Could there actually be only one giant hoax? Could these thirty-five be only one, a long-drawn-out practical joke? But how impractical for one hoaxer to spend years impersonating thirty-five persons! I have telephoned some eyewitnesses, calling their phones in various states of the country and asking them questions that would have flustered a hoaxer. In addition, some eyewitnesses have been ridiculed for maintaining the truthfulness of their experiences; a hoaxer would not endure that ridicule for long.

And what about the overall evidences against any hoax? No hoax or combination of hoaxes would have produced those statistics in featherless-descriptions, long-tails, and estimated-sizes. What hoaxer would have foreseen that I would investigate so deeply those details? No, neither many hoaxes nor one hoax were involved in the many reports analyzed in this investigation of apparent-pterosaur encounters in the United States.

Could the reports from these thirty-five eyewitnesses be the result of a strange combination of hoaxes, misidentifications, and insanity? Examine each account separately and it becomes obvious: Where does even one of them show any sign of any serious problem? Each one stands up by itself as credible, and it takes only one of these many reports to be valid, in order to prove that at least one species of pterosaurs live. The true problem is in our cultural indoctrination about the supposed ancient extinctions of all the many species of dinosaurs and pterosaurs. Actually, some have survived.

Belief in the possibility of living pterosaurs is based on something larger than the largest *ropens*: the belief in human progress, including the hope that future scientific discoveries will expand our knowledge. I believe that this expansion will include the graduation of living pterosaurs from cryptozoology into zoology. (I would be honored just to iron out the wrinkles from a robe that will be worn in that graduation ceremony.)

So how do we believe in what we have not yet seen? It begins with knowledge of one eyewitness experience, and then another, and another. Notice relationships between accounts; notice dogma in pterosaur-extinction indoctrination. Trust your feelings when you recognize the truthfulness of an eyewitness who leaves no reasonable cause for doubt, for encountering the testimony of one eyewitness is, in itself, an experience.

Appendix

Circular reasoning

In logic and mathematics, "circular reasoning" can sometimes be a useful tool, but it usually refers to a fallacy involving arguments or reasoning in common communications. That improper reasoning is called "viciously circular reasoning," and it has ensnared even highly-educated critics of the living-pterosaur investigations.

One critic ("Unexplained-Mysteries" online forum, Mar 31, 2009) said, "Simply put, if pterosaurs where [meaning 'were'] still around, they would be extremely obvious." That sounds logical, except that it was a reply to a posting that included links to many web pages on eyewitness sightings: obvious pterosaurs. Behind this comment seems to be an example of circular reasoning that I've encountered before, something like this: "Those persons could not have seen living pterosaurs because if pterosaurs were still living we would have seen them." What prevents this restatement from being circular is the difference between "those persons" and "we."

So what makes persons who report seeing living pterosaurs different from the rest of us? (What distinguishes "those persons" from us?) It's what they report, of course, and critics assume that something must be wrong with those eyewitness reports. So let's see how this creates a circle:

Live pterosaurs don't exist because no normal person has reported one -->
A person who reports one is abnormal, for live pterosaurs don't exist. ^

Why is this reasoning fallacious? It is not that the circular nature of the reasoning, also known as "begging the question," causes statements to be false, but that the apparent reasoning is not reasoning at all. Worse than worthless, it misleads in giving a false impression of logic.

Could this critic mean that modern pterosaurs, by their size and strange appearance, would be noticed by many persons? I see another kind of reasoning problem, for I've also seen no mountain lion in the mountains of Southern California, notwithstanding I've walked where mountain lions may have stalked; most Californians have never seen a wild one. If the critic's reasoning is not circular it is crooked: "Elusive" does not mean "nonexistent," and "rare" does not mean "extinct."

Later in the online forum, the same critic says, "Bit hard to miss a coastal dwelling animal of that size which need clear space to land." Whatever sighting is referred to, it seems that the main point is this: 'There could not be a large pterosaur in that area because it would have been seen there.' But that's the same fallacy of logic, for the origin of the discussion was not about the abstract concept of living pterosaurs; it was about an apparent pterosaur that was reported seen there: more circular reasoning.

I was little surprised with another brief response in the forum: "I just don't see how they could have survived into the present day without being detected." The fallacy appears the same, for how can anything be undetected when it is detected? So why don't those critics see the obvious problem ('the eyewitness could not have seen a living pterosaur because someone would have seen it')? I believe their common mistake is not from anything like a low I.Q. It's more likely they're distracted by ideas about ancient-extinction or potential-eyewitness-unreliability; mixing in old-fashioned careless thinking makes the concoction worse.

Of course those critics may have meant that we should have more than one eyewitness. But the larger postings on that thread were about many sightings, bringing up a different kind of reasoning-problem: ignoring the large numbers of sightings. That mistake, too, I have found common.

Could those critics simply be hesitant to believe that modern science could have missed modern pterosaurs? I believe that's probably part of it. But that makes it even more obvious that each of us needs to carefully watch how we think, watching out for faulty reasoning even more than some cryptozoologists watch out for modern pterosaurs. Each of us, including scientists, must guard clear thinking, or science itself will become extinct.

Still, most of the thread was positive for the possibility of live pterosaurs; nevertheless, I found nothing personally useful in this advice: ". . . please do keep in the back of your mind that Paul Nation is heavily mixed up with Jonathan Whitcomb . . ." Oh! And I thought Paul was such a great guy.

Circular reasoning is not restricted to apparent reasoning of one person. For example, person #1 says to person #2, "That cryptozoologist should be distrusted because he's heavily mixed up with John Smith." But if the "problem" with Smith is that he promotes the idea of living pterosaurs, consider: Person #2 then says to person #3, "living-pterosaur reports are nonsense because untrustworthy cryptozoologists are promoting them." If only that kind of circular reasoning were only theoretical!

That multi-critic reasoning seems to have created circularity with the reputation my associates and I have in some online forums. A vicious web site includes these key words: "Creationist Claims, Fabrications, Falsehoods, Idiocy . . . Stupid Lies, hoax. . . ." The body of the web page refers to our "delusional eyes." I find that combination of insults interesting, for one definition of "delusion" is "a false belief or opinion," and telling a lie means communicating something contrary to what the deceiver believes: an unlikely combination. But readers of that page may come to believe that something is wrong with me and my associates (concluding that one of the accusations must be true), and that may cause them to write about our unreliability on other forum pages, and that may be used to mock the concept of modern pterosaurs. The "vicious" circular reasoning is completed by the original reason that we were attacked: We proclaimed the possibility of modern pterosaurs.

The web page mentions examples of what are called "living fossils" (the Coelacanth, okapi, and megamouth shark) and says, "The only reason why . . . [they] are confirmed to be real is because we have found physical evidence for their existence." That's one thing we all agree on: confirmed-real things are, indeed, confirmed-real. But repeating examples of circular reasoning can itself make us dizzy, so what about the Coelacanth fish? Marjorie Courtenay-Latimer, in 1938, brought this living fish to the attention of the world (it was, and still is, labeled an "ancient" fish, according to standard models). Consider Latimer's experience.

After the scientific world recognized the discovery, she was praised. But what if her discovery had begun with a cryptozoological investigation? If she had first learned about the living Coelacanth through several fishermen, through only their words, should that have reflected negatively on her eventual discovery? Of course not, for scientific discovery naturally involves a trail of one person considering what another has experienced.

What if Latimer's discovery had been delayed by years of searching for the fish described to her by fishermen? Of course her eventual discovery of the Coelacanth would have vindicated her investigation. Years of work on what eventually becomes a success, afterwards rarely incites derision. But even if she had failed, even if the discovery of the fish had been made by another person, her unsuccessful search would not have made her an idiot or a liar; it would not have made her stupid or delusional.

Not that what actually happened was easy for her. She almost failed when the taxi driver saw the fish; she almost failed when the nearby museum had nothing for preserving the dead fish; she almost failed when the professor who could identify it was out of town. Although she failed to completely preserve that Coelacanth, a taxidermist preserved its outward appearance. We now credit Marjorie Courtenay-Latimer for preservation-persevering with what she felt was an important undertaking.

Indeed, perseverance in the face of temporary defeat polished the glory of the eventual success of Marie Curie, the first scientist honored with two Nobel Prizes. I am impressed by her nobility of character even more than by her intelligence, for what use is the highest mental faculty if one gives up a search before finding the success that waits beyond the next door? Many months of tedious labor eventually gave Curie her success.

Living pterosaur investigations, mostly by a handful of Americans, have given us more and more eyewitness testimonies, with limited occasional direct evidence. Critics have continued to dismiss eyewitnesses because "somebody" should have seen a large pterosaur, if they still exist. I will continue to plead for sound reasoning, until somebody captures a live pterosaur or catches one on video, notwithstanding this is taking years.

But how else is criticism of our living-pterosaur investigations related to circular reasoning? Our critics seem to imply that my associates and I are failures because we have failed to convince them; they seem to imply that nobody should take us seriously, yet they write countless paragraphs of web pages to convince people to ignore us; they imply that they've uncovered our hopelessness, yet we continue to hope and work for some discovery. If that reasoning is not circular it is curiously circuitous.

The Mesozoic objection

What about the "Mesozoic" objection? One critic declares that a lack of "post-Mesozoic remains" (no fossils in "less-ancient" rock strata) proves a pterosaur could not live in modern times. But a subtle form of circular reasoning lies buried within this declaration about fossil rocks.

When a creature thought to have lived only in the Mesozoic time period is found in a stratum, what happens? That stratum is labeled "Mesozoic." So if a pterosaur fossil causes a stratum to be "ancient," what can be reasonably concluded about an apparent lack of any pterosaur fossils in rocks not labeled "ancient?" Not a lack of modern pterosaurs. Standard-model labeling of strata relies a great deal on the axiom of ancient extinctions of certain organisms, and axioms are assumptions, not proven facts.

Could my associates and I be mistaken about this potential circular reasoning involving pterosaur fossils? It's no secret that a stratum with fossils has often been dated by a fossil it contains. What paleontologist would date any stratum as "post-Mesozoic" when it contained a *Rhamphorhynchoid* pterosaur fossil? Who would dare suggest that the creature died a few thousand years ago? Standard procedure forbids it. But that very procedure sets up circular reasoning. Here is the problem:

Pterosaurs are ancient, so their fossils certify rock layers are ancient -->
Only ancient layers have pterosaur fossils, so pterosaurs are ancient ^

I know that standard procedures in paleontology include dating methods other than fossil classification. But that remains irrelevant to this version of circular reasoning, as long as the "possibility" of a "post-Mesozoic" pterosaur fossil remains officially (even if unspokenly) forbidden.

I once communicated briefly with a skeptic who had written a web page on his doubts about living pterosaurs. Glen Kuban, a paleontologist, had done extensive investigations to support standard paleontology in the face of apparent revolutionary threats from the creationists who propose that dinosaurs and pterosaurs lived in human times. But by the end of May, 2009, his web page still included this faulty reasoning: "Based on fossil evidence, namely the lack of any known post-Cretaceous [late Mesozoic] pterosaur remains, most scientists believe pterosaurs went extinct with the dinosaurs over 65 million years ago." I don't dispute Kuban's skills in standard paleontology; I do dispute this assumption of extinction. And I will continue to publish the truth about this faulty reasoning as long as outspoken paleontologists continue to display pterosaur fossils as if evidence for extinction. Fossils are evidence for life, whenever they lived.

Philosophy at the foundation

We creationist living-pterosaur investigators, although mostly belonging to different churches, agree that the hand of an intelligent Creator can be recognized in the life of this world and in the life of God's word in scripture. How does religious philosophy or world-view relate to live pterosaurs in America? A deep subject requires a deep look; let's briefly look deeply.

Happiness may come more readily to one who is given a choice between world-views and chooses the better; but how common for one to see only one perspective, one explanation for who and why we are! While considering the possibility of extant pterosaurs, be aware that many Americans are offered a choice between hotly contested points of view, and some persons, on both sides, have condemned those on the opposite extreme. Belief and disbelief in God fight at the extremes; how and why we believe or disbelieve often just sit across the room, so consider for a moment the conflict between the philosophy at the foundation of the General Theory of Evolution and the philosophy of belief in a creative God, then please note that our happiness may rest on discussing common ground across a living room, not dragging a wounded prisoner across a battle field.

Expeditions to find living pterosaurs have been creationist expeditions, with few exceptions. A creationist believes that God created the universe, including this world of life. (I believe earth-age is secondary, at most, notwithstanding what is written under "Ropen" on Wikipedia) Most of us who have explored tropical rain forests in Papua New Guinea, searching for pterosaur-like animals, have done so with hope that humans will find God, even if we fail to find overwhelming proof of living pterosaurs.

But the labels "evolutionist" and "creationist" have been used as insults by some of those who support extreme positions. In addition, those labels have sometimes been used in ways that distort what individuals believe. It seems best to consider three simple examples of belief, remembering that individuals can choose one, or none, or a variation.

Charles Darwin chose an extreme dedication to Naturalism philosophy; his Common-Ancestry ideas seem to make God unnecessary. He chose atheism, but most Americans reject the idea that life arose without any creative act of God.

Some who believe in the existence of God also believe that the creation of life involved Darwin's Common Ancestry, meaning macro-evolution, the General Theory of Evolution. I have encountered few relevant writings or reasonings of those who believed that God created life through hundreds of millions of years of macro-evolution. I do know of serious problems with that concept, serious enough that I doubt that any believer in it has thought deeply enough about the ramifications. I think those who believe that way have little desire to delve deeply into the issues, preferring to avoid heated conflict by adopting a simplistic compromise.

What is I. D.? From the site www.intelligentdesign.org, we read, "certain features of the universe and of living things are best explained by an intelligent cause, not an undirected process such as natural selection." This can hardly itself be called a religion, since persons of many diverse religions and religious beliefs work in perfect harmony using this approach.

The Intelligent Design movement has been called, by some critics, just a new name for creationism. But objective reasoning refutes that idea, for Biblical creationism is based on belief in the Bible, and I. D. has no scriptural or creedal foundation; other critics admit that it differs from creationism. I suspect that those who try to persuade the world that I. D. equals creationism are mostly outspoken atheists who feel threatened by both movements: If courts rule that they are the same thing, I. D. research can more easily be dismissed as "religious," and therefore not "scientific."

What about creationism? Almost all living-pterosaur investigators who explored in Papua New Guinea from 1993 through 2006 are creationists, believing that God placed life on this earth only a few thousand years ago, according to human-lineage accounting from the Old Testament. The first non-creationist expedition was by *Destination Truth*, in early 2007, resulting in a mid-2007 broadcast of their *ropen* episode. But the influence of the earlier creationist explorers on living-pterosaur research is immense.

Our greatest opposition has come from outspoken critics who have been offended by our creationism. But why should those with different religious beliefs deride our efforts? Without cryptid-hunting creationists, little progress would have been made: no investigations in the southwest Pacific or in North America. Nothing would have happened; nobody else cared.

Not all Christian creationists have identical beliefs. I am one of a minority who believes in both a young life on earth (regardless of earth age) and an old universe. A common ground for Christian creationists, however, is the Biblical account of Noah: a world-wide flood. This I too believe.

MonsterQuest "Flying Monsters"

To begin, I am grateful that the History Channel's *MonsterQuest* episode on "flying monsters" in Papua New Guinea revealed to many Americans the living-pterosaur searches by Garth Guessman and Paul Nation; but the *MonsterQuest* expedition on New Britain Island, in early 2009, was not itself a serious living-pterosaur investigation but a show that cast doubt on that belief of those two Americans. I found it interesting: The episode's creators found ways to avoid the deeper beliefs of those two, never mentioning why those two talk about and search for living pterosaurs, and video footage from previous expeditions was shown with little mention of those expeditions. Nevertheless, this episode introduced many Americans to the possibility of extant pterosaurs. In that sense, it was a success.

I had assisted two of the production researchers with early pre-production, answering questions by emails and short phone conversations, notwithstanding the show's title, "MonsterQuest," made me suspicious. I made it clear in the beginning: My financial condition prevented me, or might hinder me, from going with them on their expedition. They chose Guessman, who was better prepared and knew about recent eyewitness reports in one area of Papua New Guinea. I'm glad they chose my friend.

And I'm grateful that viewers of the June 3rd episode were introduced to Guessman and Nation (two of the most-active explorers searching for living pterosaurs), for the complete truth will eventually come out, regardless of present limitations: I noticed limitations in the knowledge and understanding of the show's writers or editors.

But how does this early-2009 expedition on New Britain Island relate to reports of live pterosaurs in America? It's in a conflict between two popular philosophies in Western society: Naturalism versus Biblical creation, which relates to the conflict between extinction-ideas and extant-pterosaur ideas. If we fail to understand those two conflicts, the wonderful creatures that can fly literally in our own backyards could remain elusive for many more years. But their discovery need not take long: In Papua New Guinea, one well-funded seven-week expedition could suffice.

The "Flying Monsters" episode was created with the assumption that standard models of evolution are scientific fact. So who'd be shocked by that? The General Theory of Evolution (GTE) is portrayed by many documentaries and shows as if fact, and we in the United States are constantly exposed to biological models that were originally created on Naturalism philosophy, even while the entire combination is now labeled "science." But most of the Americans featured on this show are creationists: They reject GTE, and that fact was carefully hidden by the episode's creators.

From 1993 to early 2009 at least eight American creationists, in at least nine expeditions, (usually one or two Americans at a time) have explored carefully selected places in Papua New Guinea, searching for living pterosaurs and eyewitnesses. But why have we gone to so much trouble, sometimes draining family savings accounts or refinancing homes? After all, supporters of Darwin's General Theory of Evolution can easily explain away a living pterosaur as just another living fossil, like the Coelacanth. I will speak for myself: Objective evaluation of why we have extant pterosaurs favors the Bible's Genesis-Flood dispersal-of-life (with markedly-limited common ancestry) over the unlimited-common-ancestry idea of Darwin. Living fossils, both Coelacanth and pterosaur, harmonize better with Genesis than with macro-evolution. Charles Darwin himself understood the "problem" of living fossils and the basic principle is unchanged.

Now for the show's content. Impressive 3-D animations of giant *pterodactyloids* give no hint that many important eyewitness testimonies clearly include long tails. I realize the constraints involved with a one-hour episode: little time for distinguishing between sightings of the long-tails *Rhamphorhynchoids* and the short-tailed *Pterodactyloids*. But the World War II veteran Duane Hodgkinson is briefly interviewed, giving viewers the impression that he saw something similar to that 3-D creature.

The day after the broadcast, I talked with Garth Guessman on the phone. He told me that eyewitness reports on New Britain Island are of short-tailed creatures, rather than long-tailed ones common elsewhere in Papua New Guinea; that justifies the producers. But other things made it difficult to imagine how the producers could have been justified in their decisions.

The show begins with narration, then a native says, "[We] believe [it is] one of the spirits from our ancestors." Four Westerners then comment on the danger and adventure and the giant size of some pterosaur fossils. The narrator continues: "Now *MonsterQuest* sets out on a dangerous journey, searching for the legendary flying monsters of Papua New Guinea." An exciting introduction is standard for this kind of television show; but a documentary on eyewitness sightings this is not, for details are limited.

Perhaps the underlying philosophy of the producers of all *MonsterQuest* episodes is revealed by their introductory narrative: "Witnesses around the world report seeing monsters; are they real or imaginary? Science searches for answers." A common usage of the word "science" means that nothing contradicting Naturalism philosophy is allowed. The show seems to indicate that this is what they mean by "science:" No Creation ideas allowed.

Guessman wrote a contract to ensure that the creationist beliefs of the earlier explorers would be acknowledged. That contract was signed, but the producers fulfilled only about two or three of the eight points specified, and they were fulfilled in a way that hid Guessman's beliefs. I found nothing in the show that even hinted that there was such a thing as creationism.

Some viewers of this episode may have become convinced that evidence for living pterosaurs is scarce. Why? The eyewitness testimonies, scarcely covered, were overshadowed by a fossil-expert's declaration about ancient extinctions and his personal disbelief in extant pterosaurs. Truth would have been better served with more coverage of the eyewitness evidence, rather than the overemphasized personal doubts of that man.

The world's greatest expert on chickens—that's a fox. The details of that expertise culminate in picking bones, executed differently than, but for the same purpose as, the work of a fossil expert: to make a living. The hope differs: The paleontologist searches for ancient bones somehow protected from the destructive forces of time; the fox, for fresh meat, somehow unprotected by the farmer for a time. Interminable dogmatism keeps both of them searching: one for death anciently; the other, death soon-to-be.

We trust no fox to analyze the automatic switch that turns on the electric fence protecting chickens; why trust a paleontologist to analyze reports of live pterosaurs, for supporters of that idea appear to threaten standard paleontology? Both fox and paleontologist have specialized knowledge, with each specialization tied to its own dogma. Trust neither one outside.

I doubt that many viewers of the *MonsterQuest* episode recognized the problem with asking a paleontologist about reports of live pterosaurs. But the problem is larger than just the knowledge (or ignorance) of the paleontologist) in how to interview, and hot to analyze testimony. How could such testimony be presented to him in a way allowing him to make any objective evaluation? Working for much of his life under the assumption of ancient extinctions of pterosaurs—that, for objectivity, is a problem.

I found evidence, but not proof, for a more subtle attempt to cast doubt on eyewitness testimony. A native was shown describing the flying light to Guessman: ". . . between nine to ten o'clock when I saw that flying thing. . . . I saw a light running from down there towards the sea." (He meant a light flying.) A night shot of an island coastline is then shown while the narrator says, "He says the beast lights up large areas." Some viewers may have been mislead here, for that shot includes the blinking of a harbor buoy light, with other slightly-brighter village lights to the right.

My experiences in professional videography have taught me to be aware of subtle communications. I had been a forensic videographer, serving court trial attorneys; it was my business to catch and point out potential subliminal messages in video recording and editing. Of course a buoy light does not fly through the air; but I wonder how many viewers neglected to read the subtitles, failed to understand all the native said, and missed the point, thinking the native may have seen a light on, rather than flying towards, the sea. Few viewers would be conscious of this subtle implication.

Those viewers who carefully considered that native's testimony would have dispelled any potential conflicting connotation by that shot of the harbor light; unfortunately few viewers will view carefully. And those who methodically kept native legends and native eyewitness accounts separate would have dispelled another potential stumbling block: taking everything natives say about the *ropen* as equally valuable; unfortunately few viewers will think methodically while watching television at night. The writers and editors of this kind of television show may have more power over what we come to believe than we're comfortable to admit.

Nevertheless I'm grateful that several eyewitnesses were interviewed and Guessman's belief in the possibility of living pterosaurs was obvious. But also obvious was the promotion of a non-pterosaur explanation.

An "unknown species of bat" is what the writers of this episode seem to believe explains the "demon flyer" (the word "ropen" is rarely mentioned on the show). The narrator says, "The island harbors some of the largest bats in the world. . . . have a wingspan that can reach six feet." The music prepares us while he continues, "The team spots the roost . . ." (timpani drum rolls) . . . We see a tree full of *flying fox* fruit bats (of course: nobody yet has video footage of giant living pterosaurs). How dramatic!

About one minute of the show is spent talking about the fruit bat and scaring many of them out of a tree. Mind you, I'm delighted that parts of our world are often covered by the shadows of numberless giant fruit bats (and I enjoy professional background music in a documentary); I bask in the memory of my own first encounter with wild *flying foxes* in the southwest Pacific. But how does this bat relate to a much larger creature that glows? How does this fruit bat relate to a flying creature that is said to have picked up a native man, lifting him into the air?

The episode included a dramatization, with Guessman as narrator, of the "1986" attack by the *demon flyer*. Near Finschhafen, while a man was gardening, the creature killed him and carried his body into a tree. What the episode did not include was the supporting evidence of similar reports from other areas in Papua New Guinea; I believe that this similarity with other reports of attacks on humans is non-coincidental. The point? The large size of a fruit-eating bat does not suggest that a giant flying predator should be a bat; they are simply two different featherless flying creatures.

It seems to me that valuable air time was wasted promoting the "unknown-species-of-bat" hypothesis, for they instead could have delved into details of eyewitness accounts. The fossil expert gave not even a hint about any fossil of that "unknown bat;" the eyewitnesses gave not even a hint that they had seen that "unknown bat." *MonsterQuest* gave no evidence that the *ropen* is an unknown bat. But previous expeditions have given us evidence that the *ropen* is a *Rhamphorhynchoid* pterosaur: reports of tail movement that correspond to the anatomy of *Rhamphorhynchoid* tails, overall body-shape that was twice identified with a test-silhouette of a *Sordes Pilosus*.

Details distinguish lightning from the lightning bug. The creators of this *MonsterQuest* episode seem to have neglected some critical details, namely the results of detailed interviews in previous expeditions. Did the researchers in pre-production dig deeply enough? Was the fossil expert informed of the report about *ropen* tail movement? Did he know that two of the better sightings on nearby Umboi Island resulted in a connection with a sketch of a *Sordes Pilosus Rhamphorhynchoid*? Those details relate to fossils of long-tailed pterosaurs, and a long tail is often reported in giant flying creatures in Papua New Guinea, details absent from this episode.

Generalized bigness, nocturnal flights, lack of feathers—those similarities between *ropens* and fruit bats blush in comparison with the major differences. We could just as well compare big flying machines: a manned hot-air balloon and a manned space vehicle, both hotly launched with hot air, by adventurers of the same species. The long nose of a large anteater does not make a giant elephant an anteater (notwithstanding both are mammals). In Papua New Guinea, a gardener sometimes eats a fruit bat; but something else—entirely different—that is what sometimes eats a gardener.

The expedition itself, a trek into a remote area of the tropical forest, was impressive: twenty-five native porters, and a few Westerners, hiking more than ten miles up a slippery trail to a narrow mountain ridge. But the team spent little time searching the night sky on that ridge; they were there to film a show, not to conduct a serious scientific investigation. (Guessman's longer expedition, in 2004, was far more successful in gaining knowledge about the *ropen* of Umboi.) The *MonsterQuest* expedition created material for an entertaining show, introducing the possibility of living pterosaurs to Western television-viewers. Balance its lack of scientific research and investigation with what it did best: *MonsterQuest,* in that one-hour show, may have exposed the living-pterosaur possibility to more persons than I have, in seven years, exposed the probability. I think we're better for that.

What would be the ideal documentary on living pterosaurs? One of two directions: searching for the truth in eyewitness testimonies or searching diligently for the creatures themselves. The "Flying Monsters" episode of *MonsterQuest* did neither, stumbling by stepping on the edge separating one stair from another. Nevertheless, the lively style, the professional production values, the expedition to a remote wilderness, the balancing of opinions about the creatures—all combined for a fascinating show that introduced many Americans to the possibility of living pterosaurs in Papua New Guinea: not an ideal intellectual feast but a tasty timely snack.

"Flying Monsters" did prove one thing: Some persons in our Western society will oppose "live pterosaur," when the idea comes up. But remember, the popularity of ancient-extinction ideas among educated supporters of standard models is not, in itself, evidence for ancient extinction of pterosaurs: It is the result of a deep, long-term indoctrination.

I was gratified that the last person interviewed was Guessman. He said, "I think a lot of cryptozoological creatures, mystery creatures around the world, are simply not found because they're not looked for, and people are not expecting to find them, so they don't bother even paying attention to people that report them. They just dismiss them as some anomaly . . . something else: anything but what they're obviously telling us it is." Thank you, Garth; I heartily agree.

Paiva report about Nation video

Late in 2006, Paul Nation explored a remote mountainous area deep in the interior of the mainland of Papua New Guinea. He witnessed several *ropen*-like lights that the local natives call "indava," and videotaped two of them, just before they took off and apparently flew behind the nearby ridge. Soon after Paul returned to the United States, I flew to Texas to interview him in his home. He gave me an exact digital copy of the video; I later made another digital duplicate, which I gave to Guessman who gave it to Clifford Paiva, a missile defense physicist in California.

In 2007, Paiva wrote a scientific report, after much analysis of the video. The introduction includes, ". . . image processing utilized SCION Corporation's Advanced Image Processor (also used by the U.S. Naval Research Laboratory and by U.S. Naval Surface Warfare Center, Dahlgren . . .). . ."

The 41-page report included estimating the size of the two slowly pulsating lights. This was done after magnifying the daylight video that Paul Nation had recorded of the same ridge. A tree trunk on that ridge was estimated to have a trunk diameter of 0.9144 meters. Paiva calculated the size of the two lights, in meters of diameter: "Source 1" was 0.914; "Source 2" was 1.143. I later calculated that the smaller of these two lights was about 90 times larger than a typical firefly. Even if the tree-trunk size estimate were wrong by a factor of three (unlikely, but that would be about 0.3 meter), no firefly imagined would have a glowing abdomen one foot long. These two lights were obviously not fireflies.

With advanced image processing software and his professional skills in missile defense, Paiva found the faint background in Nation's nighttime video. He determined that the lights were stationary throughout the recording. Apparently Nation's camcorder was turned off just before the two lights flew off of the ridge, recording only 17 seconds of video.

Paiva found that the two apparent light sources were indeed two separate lights. Immediately eliminated were fires, meteors, and aircraft. He also eliminated camera artifacts: "camera inherent diffraction sources: internal camera imaging artifacts on the focal plane: <u>none</u>." Regarding hoax potential, he recorded, "potential of hoax: <u>none</u>."

On page 27 of the report, he recorded this: "Blur functions have increased which may indicate atmospheric turbulence along the LOS [line of sight]. In addition to blur function generation as a function of the index of refraction of the atmosphere along the line-of-sight, the presence of transient rise in intensity . . . removes the possibility of 'cutting' and 'pasting' external frames into the imagery. . . ."

We found it interesting that the centers of the two lights were markedly dimmer in intensity: obviously they were not produced by any car headlights or flashlights (which are brighter in the center).

In addition, Paiva determined, through computer processing, that the two lights make sense as real-world (three-dimensional) objects. Unfortunately the recording quality was insufficient to show the form of the sources: We still needed to rely on eyewitness reports of the pterosaur-like appearances of the large featherless flying creatures in Papua New Guinea. But Paul Nation's seventeen seconds of video appear to be the first images (of what we believe show the bioluminescence of giant living pterosaurs in Papua New Guinea) to be brought back to the United States.

Eskin Kuhn's sighting in Cuba

How rare the *ropen* pair, in daylight, daring sortie in the air! Notwithstanding rarity, two long-tailed intruders flew over the U.S. military base at Guantanamo Bay, Cuba, mesmerizing the marine Eskin Kuhn. The eyewitness, now living in Ohio, I interviewed early in 2010, by phone.

How fortunate that Eskin Kuhn was the marine who stood outside the new barracks on a particular sunny day around mid-July, 1971! While the other marines were hanging out inside, this talented artist was enjoying the lovely weather and looking out toward the ocean. He would soon be dashing inside to grab a sergeant to be a second witness (too late), and would soon thereafter sketch, by memory, what he had seen with his own eyes.

I here include, for good reason, the sketch drawn by this marine. It's not a substitute for a photograph; he himself recognized his lack of perfection in portraying in detail all that he had experienced. Still, when combined with

his words, it reveals the undeniable: He witnessed neither bird nor bat, for what flew before him were two long-tailed pterosaurs.

Consider the experience of Eskin C. Kuhn through his own words.

"I am an artist with sharp eye for detail and was determined to drink in the visage before me for future recording on paper. I saw two pterosaurs (or pterodactyls . . . what's in a name?) flying together at low altitude, perhaps 100 feet, very close in range from where I was standing, so that I had a perfectly clear view of them.

"The rhythm of their large wings was very graceful, slow, and yet they were flying and not merely gliding . . . The rate of their [wing flaps] was more like that of crows, perhaps a little slower, but very graceful."

The marine observed details, later recording them in his sketch: The head was large in proportion, with a large head crest; the short "hind legs" were attached to the trailing part of the wings; the vertebrae were noticeable; the end of the tail had a "tuft of hair."

He recognized the difficulty in judging size accurately, with no close point of reference in the sky, but he estimated the wingspan at about eight to twelve feet. The creatures were flying inland, from the direction of the sea; that brings up questions about where they had come from and why.

He has maintained for decades the truthfulness of his experience. At 8:50 a.m. Ohio time, on February 26, 2010, I surprised Mr. Kuhn with a phone call. He responded with something like, "It was a long time ago." I asked him questions that would have flustered a hoaxer, but they were natural, open-minded questions that would cause no offense to an honest person. Mr. Kuhn took no offense. I believe him.

He recalls other days: exploring the coast, swimming with other marines and entering a cave filled with bats; he never again saw anything like those two pterosaurs. The sighting later gained some attention on the internet, so many readers may have come to believe, with good reason, his encounter with two pterosaurs. But not everyone came to believe.

Late in 2009, a blogger going by "Abyssal" wrote six lines including, "I had been planning on writing a post called 'Thoughts on Eskin Kuhn's Pterosaur Sighting' wherein . . . an American soldier . . . saw a pterosaur while stationed in Cuba. The claim is a hoax. I no longer have the patience for dealing with creationist-related debunkings and I have no intention of actually writing up one . . ." That post deserves attention here.

On more than one level, that blogger seems to lack either clear thinking or deep thinking in that post. Perhaps by "dealing with creationist-related debunkings" that writer meant "debunking creationist ideas," for when someone talks of a hoax, "debunk" normally refers to showing how or why something is a hoax. But that blogger writes of an intention to write nothing on the subject, basically just proclaiming that the pterosaur sighting is a hoax, and we are given no reason to believe that opinion.

Did Abyssal the blogger believe there was no such person as Eskin Kuhn, that not just pterosaurs but the U.S. Marine himself was unreal? Then why include a link to a long web page that contains over 800 words of text, the words of Eskin Kuhn himself? That page also includes photos, including one of Kuhn, on the military base, holding a rifle. For those who have seen that page, belief in that young man's existence is easy, even if belief in the existence of modern pterosaurs is hard. But still Abyssal apparently doubted Kuhn's existence, for why else would he (or she) write so little about this account, yet mention that "Eskin Kuhn" was spelled differently on other web pages? It makes the marine seem unreal.

I am glad that Abyssal allowed the online publication of the first comment on that post, for it was from a U.S. Marine: fully existent Mr. Kuhn: "It is not a hoax. You weren't there. I was! I have no patience for . . ." Well, he mentioned the critic's lack of intelligence and lack of authority; enough said. No doubt Abyssal then had no doubt about the existence of Mr. Kuhn. Abyssal's response to that comment I found interesting.

[March 10, 2010] "Relax, bro, I was *not* going to do a debunking of your alleged sighting. [Abyssal then proclaims that Kuhn needs to obtain a pterosaur specimen] . . . until then, all you have is an unlikely anecdote."

I was struck by that word: "anecdote." Almost any definition includes something like "short account of an incident;" the word originated from Greek: "things unpublished." So how does that word apply to that other blog publication, the online-published page with over 800 words describing what happened before, during, and after the sighting? And what about another definition: "a secondhand account?" Kuhn's detailed account is firsthand, in his own words. No definition of "anecdote" applies here.

Abyssal took no responsibility for falsely accusing Kuhn of a hoax but instead jumped off the witness stand, marched across the courtroom, and challenged a former witness. I make no accusation of criminal conduct for that, but I point to the impropriety, for that former witness is visiting from another courtroom down the hall where another trial is in recess.

Two separate court cases this resembles: Abyssal accuses those involved with that 1971 sighting report (a hoax-accusation); Kuhn and I call him to account for a wrongful accusation. We point out the lack of any evidence for any hoax in the first case; Abyssal seems to drop that case, although seeming to avoid a real apology. We confront Abyssal in the second case (damaged reputation of a marine); Abyssal tries to avoid that by demanding that Kuhn obtain a specimen of a modern pterosaur (later making a similar challenge to me, in another blog comment). I submit that Kuhn and I have won both cases. The insinuation that Kuhn or I should obtain the body of a modern pterosaur—that bears no resemblance to any case.

Challenging an eyewitness (or an interviewer) to produce the body of a modern pterosaur is not original; a published explanation for why that challenge involves faulty reasoning, however—that is more rare than that pterosaur. The critics fail to see process-of-discovery, for cryptozoology leads the way; biology, with examinations in a laboratory and observations in the field, follows, at least with modern pterosaurs.

But how critical are individual components! The piston cannot say to the fuel injector, "I have no need of you;" nor the tire to the steering wheel, "I have no need of you." In a society that indoctrinates young children into universal extinctions of all species of dinosaurs and pterosaurs, how can anything like a dinosaur or pterosaur be discovered? It's difficult but not impossible. We must listen to the eyewitnesses; that comes first. Examining a specimen comes later, but how critical our need to first listen!

Why not challenge Thomas Edison to explain why the gravity of the sun bends the nearby passage of light from distant stars? Why not challenge Albert Einstein to invent a better light bulb? Those challenges would cast no doubt on the validity of past discoveries or inventions, for those accomplishments are documented in the past; they are history. The discovery of modern pterosaurs is in process; critical parts live in the future, and even the official acknowledgement, among biologists, of one living species (in one area of the world) will not complete that process, for a number of species now live on this planet. We have a long way to go.

Who would have challenged Nicola Tesla to fund the alternating current generator at Niagara Falls? It was enough for him to invent three-phase alternating-current generation; a monument at Niagara Falls testifies of his accomplishment: giving light to the human race, for a century. Who is Abyssal to challenge an eyewitness to produce the body of a modern pterosaur? It was enough for Eskin Kuhn to tell us what he experienced; his sketch testifies of those two pterosaurs, and the power of his testimony has enlightened at least a few persons, for four decades.

We live no longer in 1971, when Mr. Kuhn first began telling people about his sighting of those two pterosaurs in Cuba. In that year, when he drew his sketch of those two long-tailed pterosaurs with head crests, how could he have foreseen other eyewitness testimonies decades in the future? In the 1990's, a few Americans interviewed natives on Umboi Island, Papua New Guinea; other Americans followed in the early twenty-first century, searching the jungles for large nocturnal flying creatures. Eyewitness testimonies confirmed earlier testimonies: large featherless winged creatures with long tails; some eyewitnesses described a head crest. This shows Mr. Kuhn's encounter to be part of a larger pattern of human experience.

Abyssal's words do not insinuate that Kuhn's sighting was recent, but the accusation of a hoax certainly appears to come from the old dogma of the universal extinction of all species of dinosaurs and pterosaurs, and that 1971 account has stood the test of time: Nobody has come up with any evidence of any hoax, but the marine's recent words vindicate his honesty. I do not accuse Abyssal of atypical ignorance, for the popularity of extinction ideas is unquestioned; that blogger has been caught up in a popular belief that is faulty. I suggest people recognize the dogma for what it is. The marine's words and sketch do not prove modern *Rhamphorhynchoids* are still flying over Cuba, but many recent similar sightings merge with his, making that possibility so obvious that dogmatic denial is foolish.

Abyssal, what explanation do you give for Kuhn's experience? Do you insinuate insanity? What about Brian Hennessy's experience? In 1971, the same year as Kuhn's sighting, the Australian watched a large creature fly overhead on Bougainville, Papua New Guinea. It was more than a lack of any sign of feathers that brought the word "prehistoric" to his mind: The creature had a long tail and a long pointed head crest. Nobody doubts the mental health of Hennessy, for he is a professional psychologist; why doubt the sanity of this marine who sketched the same kind of creature?

Long-tailed featherless flying creatures are seen in many areas of the world. The two observed by Mr. Kuhn resemble many others, contrary to Kuhn's original notion that his sighting of a long-tail was contrary to the norm. Rarity seems to apply more to eyewitnesses-who-talk than to long-tailed pterosaurs that fly. I'm still anxious for the next email or phone call.

Living Nightmare: Attack in the Dead of Winter

From: http://www.livingpterosaur.com/blog/ (posted March 13, 2010)

The Nightmare

Remember your worst nightmare? Were you glad to wake up? Be grateful. In the early morning hours of February 23, 2010, a few miles or so south-west of Marfa, Texas, the victims were terrified by what awakened them. I am not the eyewitness, but a few days after this event, I interviewed my friend James, who had been driving through Southern Texas; he had stopped at the *Marfa Lights* viewing platform to see whatever he could.

James did not actually see the carnage. In fact, the attack I am about to describe might be only in my imagination; my critics could surely accuse me of dreaming. Indeed, my friend saw only strange lights, flying above the fields where countless spectators, for many years, have observed the dancing *Marfa Lights*. But this night was different.

What could be worse than any nightmare? In the dead of night, you are awakened by what you fear most, glaring down at you. To humans, this monster should not even exist except in a dream. This one is real. Race out of your bedroom; it's after you. Race out the front door; it follows. Search for a place to hide; it's too late. You are exposed, surrounded by many monsters ready to feast. You have fallen into their trap. Your family is scattered, chased across the freezing countryside. You are alone. You are *Eptesicus fuscus*, a *Big Brown Bat*.

Marfa Lights, Strange Predators, and Bats

I dare not now describe to you, in detail, this attacker . . . not yet; it requires an introduction that includes the behavior of *Marfa Lights*. How they fly gives us no direct clue to the appearance of what causes them (yes, I believe they are physical things that glow). But the apparent dancing of those lights, their complex interactions with each other—that shows us they are more than just lights, and the glow and the motions may serve a purpose.

Why would one of the lights seem to divide in two? After dividing, the two lights separate, flying away from each other. They then turn back and fly towards each other, to the place where they divided. This pattern has repeated itself for years. But why? No explanation that involves inanimate objects seems even close to adequate. (I have spoken with a scientist who has investigated *Marfa Lights* for years and he is still puzzled by them.)

According to Sherlock Holmes, when the impossible has been eliminated, whatever is left, however improbable, is the answer. Marfa residents instinctively recognize an intelligence behind the dancing behavior. Don't sing their lyrics of ghosts or demons, even if the human residents are serious about spooks (which is doubtful) and even if they want the mystery solved (most of them don't). But we who have seen videos and read and heard descriptions of the light-splittings, separations, and reunions — we must recognize, for the sake of reason, what is left: intelligent direction of those dancing lights. Instead of dancing ghosts or demons, let's try a different song in the same key.

UFOs fall flat. No intelligent aliens would fly just above the bushes south of Marfa, Texas, every few weeks or so, for years beyond number; the bushes are not that interesting. The lights do suggest something like giant fireflies, but if giant insects existed they would not dance around in mating rituals every few months throughout the year. It seems that this leads us along another dirt road that ends in the same impassable canyon. Intelligent researchers have been swamped by swarms of explanations, but *Marfa Lights* appear to act intelligently, and one explanation after another has been shot down by lack of reasons for the light's behavior. Let's walk down a different dirt road, one that may lead to a bat cave in a hill south of Marfa.

How do these lights relate to bats? The *Big Brown Bat* eats insects, including, at times, those that fly around at night. What attracts many flying insects? A street light (rare in a cattle-grazing landscape) or a ranch-house porch light. What about *Marfa Lights*? They do, at times, stay in one place for a time. I do not imply that bats who can sense insects in the dark would approach a large flying creature that is glowing; *Big Brown Bats*, far from rare, may be too smart to be pinned onto an endangered-species list. The relationship between lights that dance and bats that hunt insects is a bit more complicated. But these two species do relate.

When two lights separate, over a field south of Marfa, they may leave a concentration of flying insects in that area. Be careful, Mr. Big Brown. Those two large glowing creatures have flown away, I know, and your instincts tell you to go for those bugs there. But notice that those two lights (with you in the middle) are no longer becoming dimmer; they are now becoming brighter. Don't gorge yourself for too long, little furry fellow; make it a snack to go. In the open air, you have many avenues of escape; I recommend you avoid two particular directions.

This dancing pattern of *Marfa Lights* (one light appearing to divide and separate and then the two turning back to approach each other) can thus be explained. The strange beginning of the dance is now clear: One not-yet-glowing predator chooses a glowing partner and then turns on his own glow as the two separate. They were always two objects but it appeared to us that one light had divided into two.

But what nocturnal flying predator glows brighter than a thousand fire-flies? Let's consider that night of February 23rd and ask a different question. Why was that night different?

James did not see a light splitting into two and separating, according to dance custom. Can you guess why? I would not expect *Marfa Lights* to dance on this night, for the temperature had dropped, far below freezing: no insects. So what would you do if you were a hungry flying glowing predator, for the dance is over and the refreshments table is bare? Take your friends out to eat.

Perhaps my friend was fortunate not to have seen the *Marfa Lights* up close on that night. In the dark, outside the dance hall, it was ugly. On that night, they were not flying around the bushes on the plain just south of the viewing platform; James watched them flying over the hills many miles away.

I suggest that the glowing predators had found a small colony of Big Brown Bats in a cave. It may have taken only one predator to wake them from hibernation, but ten of the predators may have had a feast when the bats flew out the cave entrance. I also suggest there may be more than one reason for the predators to glow: On this night, insects were irrelevant, but perhaps, in their frenzy in the dark, the larger predators needed to avoid colliding with each other. Perhaps this is always part of the purpose for the glowing.

Glowing Barn Owls

So what is this predator? I still dare not mention the name, and forgive me for another aside, but consider another large flying predator; it glows rarely and usually dimly, but it also hunts little furry creatures. This predator, however, (brighter than hundreds of fireflies) would not dare glow near the bright lights that were swarming over the hills south of Marfa on February 23rd. Near those hills, on that night, you would not have found a glowing barn owl.

And you'll not likely find *Tyto Alba* by looking up "bioluminescent" in the index of a biology textbook. You will find that word in a book by Fred Silcock of Victoria, Australia, and you will find a sketch of a glowing barn owl on the cover. The rare but documented glow of this bird is thoroughly explained in *The Min Min Light, The Visitor Who Never Arrives.*

Barn owls are common in many parts of the world, even though they rarely glow. Perhaps when in dire need, when furry food is scarce, does instinct kick in and bioluminescence turns on; perhaps oftener. It allows them to attract and catch insects, just enough to survive until the rodents return. Owls that glow in Australia are called "Min Mins."

In the United States, we call them *ghost lights*: the *Gurdon Light* of Arkansas, the *Ghost Light* of Masters Knob (Tennessee), and the *Hornet Light* of Missouri, and others. Many fly down railroad tracks, weaving and bobbing as if somebody were searching for something by swinging a lantern from side to side. If the glow does not help an owl catch a rodent crossing the tracks, at least that bird will not collide with another.

Disbelieve in glowing nocturnal birds if you like. It's not yet been proven, to my knowledge. But why then do barn owls have white feathers on their undersides? (Light more easily passes through white feathers.)

Dancing Flying Predators: Pterosaurs?

In contrast, the bright glowing objects that fly over open fields south of Marfa glow too brightly for owls, it seems, and their complex dances (at least in warmer weather) appear too complex for bird brains. I can imagine two or three barn owls hunting together in a haphazard way, never ten of them with occasional coordinated dances.

To the point, I do know of a nocturnal flying predator that may be hunting bats around Marfa, Texas. Its glow, in Papua New Guinea, is legendary, although it has many names and is seen in other parts of the world. We call it "ropen." That is why I, rather than Mr. Silcock or a bat expert, am writing this, and why this is published on a blog page of livingptero-saur.com rather than on savingbats.com.

I interview eyewitnesses of apparent living pterosaurs. That's what I do. I've written two books on the subject, including *Live Pterosaurs in America* [first edition]; there's little room for details here. When somebody sees what appears to be a one of these creatures, whether in Bishopville, South Carolina, or Sudan, Africa, I receive an email. (The rarity of emails from Africa I attribute to rarity of computers there, not to rarity of creatures.)

I do not proclaim that a string of evidences prove that *Marfa Lights* are living pterosaurs; I merely point out that years of research (by experts perhaps more intelligent than me) have failed to explain these dances and other strange behaviors. And when the impossible has been eliminated, whatever is left, however improbable, is . . . well . . . living pterosaurs.

###

Statistics

In Chapter 9, thirty-five eyewitnesses are referred to, almost all of whom I myself interviewed. Not included among those thirty-five were those whose reports gave insufficient information. Not included were the flying light over a river in a "remote portion of the mid-U.S.," the screeching and other noises one night in Orange County, the old California newspaper accounts, and the sighting in Cuba (outside the Unitd States).

If those other sightings had been included, it seems to me that the concept of long-tailed featherless flying creatures with pterosaur-like head crests would have been strengthened. But the addition of those few reports in the statistical analysis would have made no significant difference.

When evaluating statistics for judging the possibility of hoaxes, I gave special care to what was counted. For example, a few eyewitnesses reported more than one sighting, so number-of-eyewitnesses were counted for tail-length designation, for counting sightings is inappropriate when eyewitnesses themselves are being evaluated for hoax possibilities.

If I had found any significant problem in the data, I would share it here. I found nothing in any of the data that would cast doubt on the concept that eyewitnesses had observed actual living pterosaurs.

Index

133

144